1500 INTERESTING FACTS YOU DIDN'T KNOW

CRAZY, FUNNY & RANDOM FACTS TO WIN TRIVIA

SCOTT MATTHEWS

To Mr Stell

" We hope you don't know all of these already!

Thank you for teaching me in Yr 3 and all your fab videos, stories + facts on DOJO"

From Finley Branson :)

7 BENEFITS OF READING FACTS

1. Knowledge
2. Stress Reduction
3. Mental Stimulation
4. Better Writing Skills
5. Vocabulary Expansion
6. Memory Improvement
7. Stronger Analytical Thinking Skills

The more that you read, the more things you will know. The more you learn, the more places you'll go.

— Dr. Seuss

ABOUT THE AUTHOR

 Scott Matthews is a geologist, world traveller and author of the 'Amazing World Facts' series! He was born in Brooklyn New York by immigrant parents from the Ukraine but grew up in North Carolina. Scott studied at Duke University where he graduated with a degree in Geology and History.

His studies allowed him to travel the globe where he saw and learned amazing trivial knowledge with his many encounters. With the vast amount of interesting information he accumulated he created his best selling books 'Random, Interesting & Fun Facts You Need To Know'.

He hopes these facts will provide you with hours of fun, knowledge, entertainment and laughter.

If you gain any knowledge from this book, think it's fun and could put a smile on someone's face, he would greatly appreciate your review on Amazon.

1500 FACTS

1. In Japan, there is an S&M gym called "Himitsu No Gym," which translates to "Secret Gym." There your personal trainer is a professional dominatrix who controls your diet and workout. A trial session can cost around ¥7,800.
2. A Gallup poll from 1966 showed that 66% of Americans had an unfavorable opinion of civil rights activist Doctor Martin Luther King Junior. The percentage actually increased by 26% from the poll taken in 1963.
3. The longest video game marathon playing ever recorded was achieved by Hecaterina Kinumi Iglesias who played World of Warcraft for twenty nine hours and thirty one minutes on March 29, 2014, in Vigo, Spain.
4. In comparison to adults, babies have sixty or more bones in their bodies.
5. Although Steve Irwin is known as an animal lover, there was one in particular that he didn't like very much. During an interview with Scientific American magazine, he said that: "For some reason, parrots have to bite me. That's their job; I don't know what it is." He also confessed that one almost ripped his nose off once.
6. With over 17.3 miles (twenty eight kilometers) of corridors, the

Pentagon has a total floor area of 2,010,640 square feet (613,000 square meters).

7. The verb poop meant to produce a short blast of sound with a horn during the Middle Ages. This changed in the late 1600's according to the Oxford English Dictionary, and it meant to break wind.

8. The Australian Center for Ancient DNA found out in a study that Neanderthals would self-medicate to deal with pain. When they had pain, they would eat poplar which contains a painkiller and salicylic acid, which is the active ingredient in aspirin.

9. Bamboo flowering occurs very rarely. Some species can develop flowers after 65-120 years. The weirdest thing is that when they do flower, all plants of that one bamboo species develop flowers at the same time no matter where they are located in the world.

10. Wesley is a golden retriever from Michigan that was outfitted with braces. Due to his crooked teeth, he couldn't close his mouth or chew well.

11. Although Bobby Bonilla retired in 2000, the New York Mets are still paying him $1.19 million a year. When the team wanted to cut him and pay him the rest of his contract, Bonilla's manager made an agreement with them to pay him $1.19 million for twenty five years, starting in 2011.

12. There is a photo series created by photographer Chompoo Baritone that exposes the truth of pictures. He mocks Instagram users who prop and filter their lives to make them seem more amazing than they really are.

13. The SR71 Blackbird isn't really black, but indigo blue. It has a mixture of microscopic iron ferrite balls, which make the radar signal and heat dissipate.

14. There are some salamanders that have no lungs. They breathe entirely through their skin and the tissue lining in their mouths. In order to respire, their skin and mouths must keep moist, so they are only found in damp areas.

15. Miljenko Bukovic, a newspaper vendor from Valparaiso, Chile, adores actress Julia Roberts so much that he had eighty two portraits of her tattooed on his torso. It took him ten years and

about £1300 to get them done. In fact, he plans to get more tattoos of the star on his chest, back and arms as long as there is space and he has the money.

16. The earliest case of hearing loss documented in writing is thought to be from Ancient Egypt in 1550 B.C. In that era, people injected red lead, goat urine, olive oil, bat wings and ant eggs in the ear canal in an attempt to cure bad hearing.

17. Countries located in the Bean Belt, basically the tropics, are the main producers of most of the world's coffee, with Brazil ranked as the biggest coffee-producing country in the world.

18. A shoe made exclusively from ocean trash, including gill nets and beach litter, was released by Adidas in 2015. The company stated: "there is no shortage of material to produce this line."

19. Hamsters are able to blink only one eye at a time.

20. The entire European Union is smaller than Canada alone. In fact, Canada is thirty three times bigger than Italy and fifteen times bigger than France.

21. The New Year was celebrated between March 25 and April 1 by the French. In 1564, after the introduction of the new Gregorian calendar, the festivity was moved to January 1. Some people however resisted the change and became victims of pranks, including invitations to non-existent New Year's parties on April 1. This is why we celebrate April Fool's Day on April 1st.

22. "Charles Entertainment Cheese" is the full name of Chuck E. Cheese.

23. The largest bridge cables ever made are found in the Golden Gate Bridge. They were so long that they could actually encircle the world more than three times at the equator.

24. Taiwanese comedian named Wu Zhaonan, who is recognized by Taiwan as a national treasure, created the popular Mongolian barbecue dish. He invented it when he was running a food stall in Taipei before he was famous. He was also a recipient of the lifetime achievement award from the Lincoln Center.

25. There is a 137+ year-old secret and exclusive camp known as the Bohemian Grove that is only open to the rich and powerful

men of the world. Richard Nixon was once a member, but referred to it as "the most faggy goddamn thing you'll ever imagine."

26. John Glenn, the first astronaut to orbit the Earth, made history again by becoming the oldest man to fly in space at the age of seventy seven, on October 29, 1998. He traveled aboard the space shuttle Discovery as part of a NASA study on health problems associated with aging.

27. In May 2017, a couple from Cardiff, Wales, named Martin Sherbington and Eliza Evans got married in virtual reality, on a social network called Alt Space VR. The wedding took place at a virtual nightclub called "The Spire" and around 150 of their friends and family attended the event, many of whom wouldn't have been able to make it to a real life wedding in Cardiff.

28. The largest collection of snow globes according to the Guinness World Record belongs to Wendy Suen from Shanghai, China. As of November 27, 2016, she had gathered more than 4,059 of them; she started her collection back in 2000.

29. An extra inch (2.54 centimeters) in height correlates with earning $800 more a year, according to anthropologist Thomas Gregor, from Vanderbilt University. If you roll this amount over a thirty year period, then it would equate to earning hundreds of thousands of dollars more than someone that's only an inch shorter.

30. For around 400 years, pig-tailed macaques have been raised and trained to pick coconuts in Thailand. A male monkey can collect an average of 1,600 coconuts a day and a female can get around 600, while a human can only collect about eighty in a day.

31. Since 2007, McDonald's has been taking advantage of the used cooking oil in the UK. The leftover oil has been used as fuel for more than half of their fleet of delivery trucks.

32. Shooting the film Super Mario Brothers was so laborious that Bob Hoskins and John Leguizamo, the lead actors, would get drunk between scenes.

33. Australians have a Christmas song where Santa's sleigh is

pulled by six white kangaroos. Their names are Jackaroo, Curly, Bluey, Two-Up, Desert-Head, and Snow.

34. Pemba Dorje, a Nepalese climber and also a Sherpa, holds the record for the fastest ascent of Mount Everest. In 2004, he climbed Everest in only eight hours and ten minutes.

35. On January 25, 1979, Robert Williams became the first known human to be killed by a robot. While he was working for the Flat Rock Assembly plant in Detroit, Michigan, he was tragically killed by an industrial robot arm.

36. In 1974, when transporting the mummified remains of Ramses II, an Egyptian passport was issued, which listed his occupation as "king deceased."

37. The measles virus deletes the immune system's whole memory, leaving a patient susceptible to other infections for the next three years, according to a study conducted in 2015 by a team of Princeton researchers.

38. The print of our tongues is different for every individual, just like fingerprints.

39. Back in 2007, the Royal Canadian Mint issued the world's largest coin. It was twenty inches (fifty centimeters) in diameter and one inch (2.5 centimeters) thick. It was made of 99.99% gold bullion; it weighs 220 pounds (a hundred kilograms) and is worth an estimated $1 million.

40. Every time whales poop, they transport vital nutrients to the warm surface waters, where phytoplankton use the nutrients to photosynthesize and produce oxygen.

41. The "Intertidal Zone" is a comic book about tide pool animals written by Stephen Hillenburg, a marine biology instructor at the Orange County Marine Institute. Two years after pursuing a career in animation, Stephen developed the characters from his comic book and turned them into the show "SpongeBob Squarepants."

42. There is a twenty year old anonymous British man from Birmingham, UK, who wears a Spiderman costume at night and helps homeless people by buying them food from the supermarket.

43. In the Russian city of Yekaterinburg there is a giant granite ball which was painted to look like a giant Pokeball.

44. In southeastern Indonesia, the Korowai and Kombai indigenous tribes live in homes that are atop of trees. The houses are often built between twenty feet (six meters) and eighty two feet (twenty five meters) above the ground, but they can go as high as 164 feet (fifty meters). The reason they build them that high is to protect themselves from animal attacks, to avoid the flood during the rainy season, and to be a post guard during conflict that may occur among tribes.

45. The phenomenon of storm babies is real. During storms, barometric pressure can rise which causes some expectant women to spontaneously go into labor.

46. Homeopathy treatments in America must be labeled as "not effective" unless they are scientifically proven to work.

47. There's a Romanian woman who knitted a vest made out of her own hair. From the age of forty to sixty, she collected all the hair that fell out when she combed it, and at some point, she had enough hair to knit the item, which weighed 2.2 pounds (one kilogram).

48. Flamingos can fly at a speed of thirty five miles (fifty six kilometers) per hour when flying in a flock. They may seem a bit clumsy in flight because their long necks stretch out in front of their bodies, and their long legs dangle well past their short tails.

49. In Essex, England, they have a company that allows you to hire actors to show up at your funeral, so that you can seem more popular than you really were when you were alive. It's called "Rent-A-Mourner," and their actors can come to wakes, and tell stories as though they knew the deceased.

50. Rodents cannot vomit due to anatomical constraints. In other words, they simply aren't built with the ability to.

51. In 1928, the last conviction in the United States for blasphemy took effect in Little Rock, Arkansas, to atheist activist Charles Lee Smith. A sign in the storefront window read: "Evolution is true, the Bible is a lie, God's a ghost." He was condemned to ninety days in jail and had to pay a fine of $100.

52. On December 7, 1963, instant replay was used for the first time in sports, during a football game between the Army and Navy at Municipal Stadium in Philadelphia. The first replay aired after a simple one-yard touchdown run.

53. In cities all around the world, street dogs have learned how to navigate through traffic, wait to use crosswalks during a red light, and even ride public transportation.

54. Llamas are pack animals. They can carry up to seventy five pounds (thirty four kilograms) for up to twenty miles (thirty two kilometers). If you overload one however, it will refuse to move and it will lay down and spit or hiss at you until the load is lightened.

55. When Apple began designating numbers to employees, Steve Jobs was not happy that Steve Wozniak received number one while he got number two. He believed that he should be second to no one, so he took number zero instead.

56. "Cute aggression" is the term used to refer when thinking that something such as a puppy or kitten is so cute that you could crush it. This happens when the neurons in the brain fire and create electrical activity, which makes you more aggressive.

57. There is a magnetic journal called the Rekonect Notebook where pages can be removed, reattached, or rearranged whenever you want.

58. Rap artists Nelly has been secretly offering college sponsorships for two kids every year for the last decade.

59. In the early 1980's, a fourteen-carat gold Lego brick was given out to those employees who had worked at the Germany Lego Factory for over twenty five years. Today they are valued at over $15,000.

60. In 2015, around 2,200 pounds (1,000 kilograms) of gold were recovered by Apple from recycled iPhones, iPads, and Macs, which was worth over $40 million. Gold is highly averse to corrosion and an excellent conductor of electricity, which is why it's often used in consumer electronics. Even though silver is actually the best conductor, it corrodes more easily.

61. Getting red eyes from swimming is not actually caused by the contact with too much chlorine. According to health experts,

it's the result of being exposed to bodily fluids in the water, like urine, feces, and sweat.

62. On July 4, 1826, US former Presidents John Adams and Thomas Jefferson both died in different states from different illnesses. On that same day, the country was celebrating the 50th anniversary of their Declaration of Independence. President James Monroe also died on July 4, but in 1831. In other words, three of the five first US presidents died on Independence Day.

63. The teeth of marine snails are so strong that they are able to clamp onto rocks and grind them down as they feed. They are made from the strongest natural material on Earth.

64. The fear of peanut butter sticking to the roof of your mouth is called arachibutyrophobia.

65. Despite the huge success of the music band "The Beatles," who sold more than 1.6 billion singles in the United States, 600 million albums worldwide, and won eight Grammy Awards, not one member of the band could actually read or write sheet music.

66. In Malay, "orang" means person and "hutan" means forest. In other words, orangutan means "person of the forest."

67. Scipio Africanus was a Roman soldier who survived battles at Ticinus, Cannae, and Trasimene, all of which his country lost. He, however, ended up leading the Roman army as a general, and he defeated Hannibal, one of history's greatest military commanders.

68. Researcher James Gilpin has developed a new way to make whiskey by taking the sugar from the urine of elderly people with diabetes. He then bottles the whiskey with the name and age of the person who donated the urine.

69. The Emperor Penguin can dive up to 1,800 feet (550 meters) underwater which is deeper than any other bird. They can also hold their breath for up to twenty minutes at a time.

70. To help them swallow food, leopard frogs use their eyes. They squeeze their eyes shut, pulling them inwards toward their mouths, and this helps compress food and push it down their throats.

71. Located off the coast of Antarctica, the Elephant Island has elephant moss growing on it that is over 5,500 years old.
72. It's possible to be prosecuted criminally for making death threats written in emojis.
73. The first US states to require a driver's license were Massachusetts and Missouri, back in 1903. It wasn't necessary to pass a test however, you just needed to have one.
74. In 1982, Tylenol murders in Chicago killed seven people. No suspect was ever caught or charged for the crime.
75. In a 2014 study conducted by JAMA Dermatology, it was found that tanning caused more cases of skin cancer than the number of instances of lung cancer that were caused by smoking.
76. "Drake" is the name given to a male duck.
77. In Thailand, there is a temple called "Wat Samphran" that has a giant dragon wrapped around the outside of the building that is about seventeen stories high. On the surroundings, there are also other various animal sculptures, like an elephant, rabbit, dolphins, and other large buildings in the shape of a tortoise.
78. It's possible to purchase different wedding e-cards from Domino's pizza to give to someone. Some of the cards they offer are a $25 gift of pizza called "the post-honeymoon adjustment to real life because washing the dishes is the worst." There is also a $15 married but chill option.
79. In 1518, in Strasbourg, there was an outbreak of manic dancing known as the "Dancing Plague" that consisted of 400 people, mostly women. Over the course of one month, fifteen people a day died from heart attacks and exhaustion.
80. When exposed to certain ingredients such as sandalwood oil, our skin has the ability to smell and is even able to heal itself.
81. The music from the video game "Sonic the Hedgehog Three & Knuckles" was composed by the late Michael Jackson, who refused to take credit for the work when he heard how it sounded after it was mixed into the game.
82. According to the International Society for Photogrammetry and Remote Sensing, the largest irrigated crop in the United

States is lawn grass. Every year lawns are given so much water that it's almost enough to fill the Chesapeake Bay.

83. Actor Kurt Russell smashed an authentic Martin guitar from the 1870's during the filming of the movie "The Hateful Eight." The guitar was on loan from the Martin Guitar Museum and it was supposed to be switched out for a prop before he smashed it. Unfortunately for the actor no one told him.

84. Research done by the Australian National University found that there are more than ten times as many stars in the night sky than there are grains of sand in all the beaches and deserts in the world.

85. It's estimated that in 21% of identical twin pairs, one is right-handed while the other is either left-handed or ambidextrous.

86. On January 27, 1888, the National Geographic Society was founded with thirty-three members that included geographers, explorers, teachers, lawyers, cartographers, military officers, and financiers. All supporters had an interest in scientific and geographical knowledge and wanted to share it with everyone.

87. Samuel Langhorn Clemens was writer Mark Twain's real name.

88. To count to the number one trillion it would take you approximately 31,709 years.

89. Thousands of plastic, yellow ducks fell out of a cargo ship in the Pacific Ocean in 1992, many of which have been turning up in random locations around the world for the past twenty eight years.

90. The Journal of Positive Psychology showed that over half of all people have no clue at what their strengths are or what they're good at.

91. Nemanja Petrovic, a Serbian street beggar, realized that he was able to make more money by begging if he was not around while he did it. He made a sign that said "Invisible beggar" and tossed it on the ground with his hat and shoes, and left. When he came back, he found his hat full of money.

92. The spray that comes out of a blue whale's blowhole when it exhales can reach almost thirty feet (nine meters) into the air.

93. Our pollution has actually reached Mars. In 2012, NASA discovered a bright object on the surface of the red planet, and became intrigued as to what it could be. Later they discovered that it was a piece of plastic from the Curiosity Rover.

94. According to a study conducted by Cristel Antonia Russell and Sidney J. Levy in 2012, watching your favorite movie repeatedly can be good for you, as the repetition can calm you down. Knowing the outcome of a story helps you feel safe in an unpredictable world, as well as helps comfort you by recapturing lost feelings.

95. On January 1, 1976, a law that relaxed the use of marijuana came into effect in California. Art student Danny Finegood and some of his classmates from Cal State Northridge took $50 worth of fabric to the Hollywood sign and changed it to read Hollyweed. They used the joke as a school project, earning them an A.

96. On average, a human will produce seventy two million red blood cells, shed 174,000 skin cells, and have twenty five thoughts every thirty seconds.

97. In 1980, Saddam Hussein was given Detroit's key to the city.

98. The longest mathematical proof in history is 15,000 pages long. It involved more than a hundred mathematicians and took over thirty years to complete.

99. The first AFL/NFL World Championship game was the official name of the first Super Bowl.

100. In the 1960's, Dr. Pepper was marketed as a warm holiday drink. The idea was to heat it up in a saucepan until it lost all of its carbonation and then pour the warm and sweet beverage over a lemon.

101. In 1939, a rally of 20,000 Nazi supporters was held at Madison Square Garden, in New York City, by the German American Bund.

102. In Sydney, Australia, there is a hangover clinic. An hour treatment can cost $200 and it includes a half gallon of hydration drip, oxygen therapy, and vitamins to help you recover from a night of excessive alcohol.

103. In 1986, waterbeds were so popular that they took up 20% of

the bed market that year. These days, they make up less than 5% of bed sales. They were originally used as a form of therapy for medical patients back in the 19th century.

104. 128,437,425 miles (206,655,816 kilometer) separates Mars from the Sun at its closest point, and 154,845,701 miles (249,146,732 kilometers) at the furthest.

105. According to NASA, a trip to Mars would take about two-and-a-half years to complete. To begin with, six months are needed to travel to Mars and another six months to return. On top of that, astronauts that go would have to stay eighteen to twenty months on the planet before the planets realign for a return trip. The whole trip could cost up to $40 billion.

106. The eagle used to be a fifth playing card suit. In the United States, those cards were green with an eagle on them instead of red or black. In England, they were blue with a royal symbol for a crown. They were originally created to be used in the game of bridge.

107. In the US alone, 8,179 toothpick related accidental injuries were reported from 1979 to 1982. Additionally, three people died as a result of swallowing small bits of wood. Currently, about 9,000 people a year, most of them children ages five to fourteen, end up in American hospitals after choking on toothpicks.

108. Although baby hedgehogs are born with quills, they are actually soft and flexible.

109. Anthony Victor has the longest ear hair ever, according to Guinness World Records, measuring over seven inches (seventeen centimeters) at its longest point.

110. In Scotland, there are three verdicts instead of two under the court of law: guilty, not guilty, and not proven.

111. The record for the shortest NBA player of all time is held by Mugsy Bowes at 5'3" (1.61 meters).

112. Shigeru Miyamoto, the Super Mario creator, said that he did not like the 1993 film adaptation of it given that it was very similar to the video game.

113. "The Terminator" is the name of the line on Earth that separates day from night. Other names to refer to it include

"the gray line" and "the twilight zone." Our atmosphere also bends sunlight by half of a degree, which is 37.2 miles (sixty kilometers). For this reason, the land covered by sunlight is greater than the land that is covered by darkness.

114. In Australia, a beer was created by "Seven Cent Brewery" using the yeast isolated from the belly button lint of its brewers.

115. One in every 3,000 babies is born with a tooth.

116. On February 6, 1971, astronaut Alan Shepard became the first and only person to play golf anywhere other than Earth. He used a makeshift six iron he had smuggled on board Apollo 14 to hit two golf balls on the Moon's surface.

117. On July 20, 1944, Colonel Claus Von Stauffenberg, Chief of the Army Reserve, tried to assassinate Adolf Hitler. He planted a bomb in a briefcase which he placed near Hitler under a table, then left quickly. Another Colonel inadvertently moved the bomb further away from Hitler. When it was detonated, Hitler was injured but he survived.

118. In order to prevent your flatulence from smelling, it's possible to buy flatulence deodorizer pads. They are worn in your underwear.

119. Since 1972, artist Michael Heizer has been working on a huge sculpture in the Nevada desert. The piece of art is called "City" and covers an area of 1.2 miles (two kilometers) by 0.2 miles (0.4 kilometers). According to the artist, he got inspired after visiting Yucatan and having studied Chichén Itzá. The work of art won't be open to the public until 2020.

120. Teddy bears have caused more deaths in the last ninety years. This is because parts of teddy bears such as the eyes and nose can become choking hazards as well as being a tripping hazard for young toddlers.

121. Phong Nha-Ke Bang National Park in Vietnam is home to the largest cave in the world. The cave is big enough to fit a whole Manhattan city block on the inside, or fly an entire Boeing 747 aircraft through it. It is 21.1 miles (thirty four kilometers) long.

122. Music used to be released on a Tuesday due to shipping before the pre-digital era. After July 10, 2015, new music is now mostly released on Fridays.

123. Only one kind of snake has a pair of tentacles at the front part of its head, and it's called a "tentacle snake." The tentacles have the ability to detect vibration and pressure.

124. Pregnancy time of gorillas is the same as humans, that is, nine months. However, gorilla babies usually weigh less than human babies, about 3.8 pounds (1.81 kilograms), but their development is around twice as fast.

125. There is a restaurant in Kochi, India, called "Pappadavada" that has placed a functioning fridge outside where customers can leave leftovers for other people in need.

126. One of the best ways to retain vitamins and nutrients in food when you cook it in a microwave is by placing a small amount of water inside.

127. The U.S.S. Sequoia was a presidential yacht used from the Herbert Hoover administration until Jimmy Carter sold it in 1977. It had an elevator for Franklin Roosevelt, but Lyndon Johnson replaced it with a Liquor Bar.

128. On October 6, 1909, Vancouver unveiled its first ambulance. When they first took it for a test drive around town, it ended running over and instantly killing a wealthy man from Austin, Texas, becoming the first person the ambulance picked up.

129. On June 8, 1971, seventy two year old author J. I. Rodale died during the taping of the Dick Cavett Show. Before he died, he told Cavett that he was in such good health that he fell down a flight of stairs and laughed the whole way down. He also said that he was going to live to 100.

130. In Stanley Park, Vancouver, there is a cannon that goes off every night at exactly 9:00 pm. It was installed in 1898 by the Canadian department of Marine and Fisheries to warn fishermen that the nightly fishing was now closed. It's overlooking Coal Harbor in the downtown skyline.

131. Orcas are also known as killer whales and are actually dolphins, not whales.

132. Peter Weir, the Truman Show director, wanted to place secret cameras behind the scenes in movie theaters, so that the projectionist could cut the film at some point during the movie

and have the audience watch themselves, and then he would cut back to the movie.

133. Bagpipes are commonly identified with Scotland; however, they were actually introduced to the British Isles by the Romans.

134. In China, it's possible to buy baby pears shaped like Buddha. The farmers actually clamp a mold onto a growing fruit to get the shape. There is also a company called "Fruit Mold" that makes heart-shaped cucumbers, square watermelons, and other more deliciously weird shapes.

135. Subsix is a restaurant located around twenty feet (six meters) below the surface of the Indian Ocean, in the Maldives. You can sit near floor to ceiling glass windows and watch schools of fish and more than ninety coral reef species while you eat.

136. The first country to offer free public transit to its residents is Luxembourg. The main goal is to relieve big traffic jams for commuters as the country has the highest amount of cars in relation to its population in the European Union.

137. The study of bells and how they are cast, tuned, rung, and sound is called "campanology." It also comprises the history, methods, and traditions of bell-ringing as an art.

138. A method to use the vascular network in spinach leaves to deliver blood, oxygen, and nutrients to grow human tissue is being developed by researchers at the Worcester Polytechnic Institute. In the future, they hope to be able to use this to filter blood better to damaged tissue in the human heart.

139. In the early 20th century, Sears published and distributed tombstone and monument catalogs among Americans.

140. At the 2008 Olympics in Beijing, in order to protect the athletes from food poisoning, white mice were fed twenty four hours in advance with the same food given to the athletes. If there was a problem, the food could be traced and destroyed before being fed to the athletes.

141. The biggest fortune left to a charity was by a lady named Margaret Anne Cargill who left stocks that totaled six billion dollars.

142. The first and oldest running municipal airport in the United

States is Albany International Airport. The airstrip was first built in 1908 on an old polo field.

143. You can purchase meat from cow-bison hybrids in twenty one of fifty American States. The hybrids are called "beefalos."

144. The Wallace flying frog is known to be able to glide from tree branches and glide up to forty nine feet (fifteen meters) by splaying their four webbed feet. As they fall, the skin flaps catch the air.

145. Cats intentionally manipulate people into doing what they want, whether it's to be fed or something else. They make a special kind of purring sound that's similar to a normal purr, but has in it, a cry that people find difficult to ignore.

146. There was a violinist in the early 1800's named Niccolo Paganini that was so good that people thought he sold his soul to the devil for his talent. He was forced to show the public his mother's letters to prove that he was human.

147. Maladaptive daydreaming is a mental disorder that causes people to daydream repeatedly to escape reality. It is a defense mechanism usually caused by trauma and abuse.

148. According to historians, William Shakespeare was born and died on the same date. He was born on April 23, 1564, and he died on April 23, 1616.

149. The first century A.D. Greek tune Seikilos Epitaph is the oldest musical composition to have survived in its entirety. The song was found in Turkey engraved on an ancient marble column, and it was used to mark women's grave sites.

150. After watching the movie "Cannonball Run," Ken Imhoff fell in love with Lamborghini cars, so he spent seventeen years building a Lamborghini Countach in his basement. He eventually put the car up for sale on eBay and sold to the highest bidder in Florida for $89,000 US. It cost him $65,000 to build it.

151. A woman named Alice Pick once attempted to use a million dollar bill for a purchase that came to $1,600 in Walmart. She expected to receive all of the change too.

152. The Museo Galileo in Florence, Italy, exhibits Galileo's preserved middle finger. It stands eternally giving the bird in

the general direction of the church that once censored his theories, destroyed his good name, imprisoned him in his home, refused for nearly a century to give the man the decent burial that he was due, and for 350 years, neglected to grant him any honor.

153. Renegade was President Obama's Secret Service code name.

154. The North compounded the counterfeit problem experienced in the South during the American Civil War, when they printed large numbers of fake notes and distributed them in many southern communities. This resulted in serious inflation, which negatively impacted the economy of the confederacy.

155. The Hunger Games is banned in Vietnam. The movie was considered as too violent by the Vietnamese National Film Board, so they unanimously voted for it to be banned.

156. The only entertainer to have all five stars on the Hollywood Walk of Fame is actor-singer Gene Autry. One for radio, one for recording, one for motion pictures, one for television, and one for live theater performance.

157. Chewing gum causes you to produce more saliva, which increases swallowing, which increases the amount of air that you swallow, which makes you fart more.

158. Steve Jobs used to often eat at his biological father's Mediterranean restaurant in San Jose, California, without ever knowing that the owner was his father. They even met a few times.

159. During World War II, fashion designer Coco Chanel was a spy for the Nazi Party and an advocate during the Third Reich. She shared the idea that Jewish people were a threat to Europe.

160. Český Krumlov is a castle located in the Czech Republic that has a bear moat. The moat originally housed bears as protection, in 1707, and has been reconstructed in the 1990's, where bears were once again added to the moat.

161. In the United States, apples that are sold in stores can be up to one year old.

162. Watermelon is 92% water. It's a great choice to stay hydrated and is also low in calories.

163. Lots of Mayflower pilgrims were running away from

prosecution in England, and some others were actually leaving because they feared that the Dutch Republic was influencing their kids.

164. The wind phone is a phone booth located on the top of a hill that overlooks the Pacific Ocean and Otsuchi town in the Northeastern part of Japan. It's there to "connect" family members to their loved ones who lost their lives in the 2011 earthquake and tsunami that hit the coastline of Japan.

165. On average, women have longer legs and shorter torsos in comparison to men. Additionally, they often have shorter arms than their male counterparts.

166. MI-5 once planned to use gerbils to detect terrorists and spies at airports, given that their great sense of smell could acutely detect increased adrenaline in people. However, the project was abandoned when they noticed that the gerbils were not able to tell the difference between terrorists and those who were just afraid of flying.

167. The only place in the world where you can see the sun rise on the Pacific Ocean and setting on the Atlantic is Panama.

168. Eel's blood is poisonous, that is why it's always cooked before eating. Just a small amount of eel's blood can kill a person. In consequence, raw eel should never be eaten.

169. On the evening of September 11, 2001, a candlelight vigil was carried out by hundreds of Iranian people who gathered in Madar Square, Tehran, to express sympathy and support for the American people.

170. One of the tiniest known vertebrates is the common pygmy seahorse, or Bargibant's seahorse. It's a camouflage expert and has a maximum length of just one inch (2.5 centimeters).

171. In 2016, the oldest human fingerprint was discovered by a team of archeologists in northern Kuwait. The 7,300-year-old human fingerprint was found on a piece of broken clay pot, dating to the Stone Age, that is, 8,700 B.C. to 2,000 B.C.

172. In Italy, there are approximately 2,000 native Greek speakers today. They derive from the ancient Greek colonization on the Italian Peninsula.

173. Jukusui-Kun, meaning deep sleep, is a kind of stop snoring

pillow bot developed by Akiyoshi Kabe of Waseda University, in Japan. The polar bear shaped pillow can gauge snoring levels and will touch the snorer to get them to roll their heads to help them stop snoring. It monitors snoring with a built-in mic and a device worn around the wrist that measures blood oxygen levels, which happen to drop when the person starts snoring.

174. On July 10, 1958, a 7.7 magnitude earthquake struck the region of Alaska, resulting in a tsunami that caused the largest waves ever recorded in Lituya Bay. One of the waves measured a maximum height of 1,718 feet (524 meters).

175. There's an island called "Just Enough Room" on the Saint Lawrence River between Canada and the US, where there's literally just enough room for a tree and a house.

176. In Carnegie Hall, first-time stagehands get paid an average of $400,000 a year.

177. For thirty years, Ella Slack has been the body double for Queen Elizabeth. She actually takes the place of the queen during practices for large events.

178. In 2001, the State of Arizona passed a safe-haven law declaring that a parent is legally allowed to anonymously leave their newborn baby at a safe haven like a fire station, hospital, or church. The only requirement was that they did it in less than seventy two hours of the baby being born.

179. Racoons that live in the city are very intelligent and have adapted to their environment, learning to open doors and take lids of trash cans.

180. According to different studies, hummingbirds are able to remember migration routes as well as every flower that they have ever visited. The brain in a hummingbird makes up 4.2% of its entire weight; in proportion, it is the largest of any other bird.

181. Thirty six seconds after launch, on November 14, 1969, the Apollo 12 was struck by lightning and moments later, it was struck again. The second strike tore through the ship and wiped out many of its electrical systems. One of the flight controllers actually switched the spacecraft's signaling

conditioning equipment to auxiliary. Fortunately, the Apollo 12 was able to continue on to successfully land on the moon.

182. In 2017, the world's first hydrogen powered zero emission train was put into service by Germany. The non-electric network trains are powered using a hydrogen fuel cell, which only emits steam and water.

183. Traquair Castle is the oldest inhabited house in Scotland. It's located less than thirty miles (forty eight kilometers) from Edinburgh and it has been lived in for over 900 years. It was initially a hunting lodge for the kings and queens of Scotland.

184. Cats' eyes have a reddish glow in darkness as a result of light reflecting on a layer of tissue located inside the eyeball behind the retina, that's known as the tapetum lucidum.

185. The scientific word for picking your nose is rhinotillexomania. Rhino means nose, tillex means habitual picking, while mania means rage or fury.

186. On July 30, 2016, forty two year old paratrooper Luke Aikens became the first person to jump from an airplane without a parachute or wingsuit in California. He jumped 25,000 feet (7,600 meters) high from the ground, setting a world record for the highest jump. He safely landed in a 100-square-foot (nine-meter-squared) net, which was about one third the size of a football field.

187. In 2012, an old bridge in Wuppertal, Germany, was transformed into a massive Lego structure by street artist Megx. He used colored panels to create the illusion of the underside as Lego bricks.

188. The planet Uranus has a diameter of 31,700 miles (51,100 kilometers) across, which is four times bigger than Earth.

189. According to studies, psychopaths are immune to contagious yawning and are also less likely to be startled.

190. A system that collects AC condensation and lets you drink the water from a tap on your dashboard was developed by Ford engineer Doug Martin. The water, however, needs to first be routed through a filter that removes any organic particulate contaminants.

191. Besides Neanderthals, humans interbred with another ancient

species called Denisovans. Scientists once found a 90,000-year-old skeleton of a girl who was a hybrid between the two species.

192. Famous designer Hugo Boss used to make Nazi uniforms. In fact, he was part of the Nazi party.

193. In 2013, in an attempt to make French fries healthier, Burger King introduced satis-fries, a low calorie alternative. Customers, however, preferred the full fat version and Burger King had to dismiss the item the following year.

194. If you gather and melt down together all the gold that was ever mined in the world, it would fill about 3.5 Olympic-size pools.

195. The "Elide Fire Ball" is a fire extinguisher that you just throw or roll at the fire from a safe distance. The ball will self-activate after contacting fire for about three to ten seconds, extinguishing the surrounding area.

196. There is a gold plated Sony Walkman that costs around $3,680. It was created as the Japanese electronics giant focuses on higher end products in its audio division.

197. "Goat Song" is the classical Greek term for the word "tragedy." Scholars believe that the main prize in competitions of dancing or singing during that time was a goat.

198. The ideas for the movies "Wall-E," "A Bug's Life," "Monsters Inc.," and "Finding Nemo" were created in one meeting at the Pixar office.

199. In 1946, The United States attempted to buy Greenland for one hundred million dollars.

200. At the University of Ohio's campus, there are utility tunnels lined with pipes that run under most of the buildings. They were created in the late 1800's as a way to access the pipes in case of an emergency without digging through the lawn, and they are still in use today.

201. The only gemstone that doesn't literally belong to this world is the peridot gem. They have been spotted on comets, in large formations on Mars, and inside certain meteorites that have hit the Earth from deep space.

202. Approximately six million tons of mass are lost in the sun every second due to nuclear fission and solar winds. However, over

the last 4.5 billion years, it has only lost about 0.05% of its original mass.

203. In 1967, Florida issued a law allowing Disney World to build a nuclear power plant. Although they had never built one and have no intention to do it, the law still stands.

204. Lena Headley who plays Cersei, and Jerome Flynn who plays Bronn on the HBO Series "Game of Thrones," are never put on the same scene together because they dated in real life and had a terrible break up. They both have contracts with the show, which stipulate that they can't ever be in the same room at the same time.

205. The first transgender school has opened in Kochi, India. The school is named Sahaj International. The school aims to offer equal opportunities for transgender students, who had dropped out of other schools due to discrimination.

206. Mark Quinn is an artist that creates self-portraits using his own blood as a medium. He casts his own head in plaster mixed with ten pints of his own blood and then immerses it in frozen silicone. He has been doing this every year, since 1991, as a way to preserve the natural aging process as well as a symbol of his alcohol addiction.

207. The first time that Julius Caesar saw giraffes, he named them camelopards since they looked to him like both camels and leopards.

208. It's possible to buy toothpaste infused with caffeine that gives you a boost with your morning brush. It's found on the market as "Power Energy Toothpaste" and, unlike coffee, it takes effect almost immediately, making you more alert before you are even finished brushing.

209. Until 1964, when Teressa Bellissimo invented the buffalo wing at her restaurant in Anchor Bar in Buffalo, New York, chicken wings used to be throwaway parts of the chicken in restaurant kitchens. Today wings are actually the most popular and expensive part of the chicken in the United States.

210. Before it was popular to watch Netflix and to pause live television, EastEnders, a British television show, would cause major spikes in the country's power grid, forcing backup power

stations to come on. This happened because when it was time for a commercial break, millions of viewers would put on tea kettles at the same time, and that would draw all the electricity all at once.

211. In 1794, George Washington founded the Springfield Armory in Massachusetts. The company manufactured weapons for every major war in US history, from the war of 1812 until the Vietnam War in 1968.

212. In ancient Greece, a truce was called during the Olympics so that athletes and spectators could travel safely. No wars were permitted and no arms could be carried. Initially, the truce would last one month; but in later centuries, it was extended to three.

213. Although the population of Finland is only 5.3 million, there are approximately two million saunas in the country. People there can basically go to their favorite sauna whenever or wherever they want.

214. Like humans, koalas have fingerprints; in fact, they are quite similar to human ones. Even through careful analysis under a microscope, it's not easy to differentiate the loopy, whorled ridges on koala's fingers from our own.

215. The Guinness World Record for the highest fall survived without a parachute is held by a woman named Vesna Vulovic from Yugoslavia. On January 26, 1972, she was working as a flight attendant when the plane she was aboard blew up; she fell inside a section of the tail unit, falling over 32,800 feet (10,000 meters) over the Czech Republic. She had multiple broken bones, spent sixteen months at hospital, recovered from a twenty seven day coma, and miraculously survived.

216. In 2011, a $1 million bottle was unveiled by DKNY for its Golden Delicious perfume line. The bottle is covered in 2,909 precious stones from all over the world; each of them was hand-placed to look like the New York City skyline.

217. The most visited museum in the world in 2014 was the Louvre Museum, in Paris. It welcomed about 9.3 million visitors, almost as many people as the population of Sweden.

218. During World War II, the Pittsburgh Steelers and the

Philadelphia Eagles were combined to make one team, the Steagles, as many players were called to duty.

219. If you want to temporarily get rid of the feeling of nausea, smelling rubbing alcohol can actually help. After three or four deep breaths, the isopropyl in the alcohol pads greatly reduce nausea and vomiting.

220. It came out in 2017 that Willem-Alexander, the Dutch King, had been moonlighting as a pilot for the past twenty one years, and that he secretly co-piloted passenger flights two times every month. After his coronation as king in 2013, he chose to keep co-piloting passenger flights because he really enjoyed flying.

221. Plants of the genus Dieffenbachia are commonly referred to as "mother-in-law's tongue" because when someone comes in contact with their poison, they can be rendered temporarily speechless.

222. As a result of mismanagement, the social news site Digg was sold for $500,000. The company was once valued at $200 million.

223. There is a village in France known as "Sarpourenx," where it's illegal to die because of space restrictions.

224. The highest-ranking officer to be killed during the US Civil War was General Albert Johnston. He didn't pay much attention to a wound he got on his leg and eventually died from losing too much blood.

225. Humans put a man on the moon before they put wheels on luggage.

226. At the upper atmosphere, the Earth receives 174 pedo watts of solar radiation. About 30% of that is reflected back to space and the rest is absorbed by clouds, oceans, and land masses.

227. The highest flying bird ever recorded is the ruppell's griffon vulture. They have been recorded to fly at an altitude of seven miles (eleven kilometers) from the ground. To put it into perspective, the average commercial plane flies at about 5.5-7.4 miles (nine to twelve kilometers) in the air. The vulture, in fact, has developed a special type of hemoglobin which makes their oxygen intake much more effective at those heights.

228. John Dillinger was actually a professional baseball player before

he became a criminal and a famous bank robber. He played shortstop for Martinsville Athletics.

229. In America, citizens can mail a request to the FBI asking for the file that the bureau has on them.

230. In 2016, McDonald's in Japan started selling pumpkin spice fries. They are called the Halloween Choco-Potato; they are french fries drizzled with a pumpkin spiced and chocolate sauce.

231. A food and brand lab study of 497 diners conducted by Cornell revealed that customers who order their dinner from a heavy server ordered significantly more food, were four times more likely to order dessert, and ordered 17% more alcohol.

232. The nose prints of cats are unique as humans' fingerprints. When cat microchips become useless, nose prints can be used to identify lost cats. Additionally, a cat's sense of smell is known to be fourteen times more sensitive than ours.

233. Hydrogen peroxide is not recommended for cuts and wounds, as it slows healing by killing healthy skin cells as well as bad ones.

234. In 2013, Ed Sheeran's The A Team received a Grammy nomination. Elton John suggested having Ed give a performance opening at the awards show, but he was told he was not high profile enough. To solve the problem, Elton decided to perform with Ed.

235. The sister ship of the Titanic, Britannic, was sunk during World War I. Although the ship was greatly improved after the Titanic sank, it still sank in only fifty five minutes.

236. The first selfie photograph was taken in 1839.

237. One of the main reasons why the police still use horses today is because they offer an important height advantage. Officers can easily overlook large crowds of people as well as move through them, something that they are not able to do if they were to be on foot or in a car.

238. In 1999, actor Christian Bale played Jesus Christ in a movie called "Mary, Mother of Jesus," made for television. According to Rotten Tomatoes, it had a 48% audience score.

239. Minus forty degrees Fahrenheit and minus forty degrees Celsius

are exactly the same temperatures. Fahrenheit devised his scale using the coldest temperature that he could produce using brine as the zero point, and the temperature of the body as 100. Celsius used the freezing and boiling points of water as his zero point and 100.

240. The Auto Insurance Center decided to rank American states with the highest selfies taken while driving in 2016. After looking through more than 70,000 Instagram posts, they discovered that California had 2.53 driving selfies for every 100,000 residents, making it number one in the whole country.

241. Eggplant is actually a fruit, not a vegetable. In fact, it is considered a family of the berries.

242. Google Chrome's dinosaur Wi-Fi error message is also a game. Next time you see the dinosaur, just press the spacebar and you will see your T-rex jump. Try not to let him land on the cactus or it'll be game over.

243. Dalmatian puppies are usually born with solid white coats. The spots are invisible and they appear when the puppies are about ten days old.

244. The Hogwarts Express is a real train that you can ride in Scotland. The name of the train is "The Jacobite" and is also known for running on the most beautiful railway route in the UK.

245. Discovered in the 1920's, the Nazca Lines are ancient geoglyphs found in southern Peru that span over 321.6 square miles (518 square kilometers). They have more than 800 straight lines, 300 geometric figures, and seventy animal and plant designs, which are only appreciated in full from air.

246. "Ear furnishing" is the term used to refer to the fur that grows on the inside of the ears of cats.

247. In Germany, there are elevators with no doors; they are called paternoster elevators. They go floor to floor on a loop and you can just hop out when you get to your floor.

248. Mike Tyson, the former heavyweight champion, has a hectic daily workout schedule. He gets up at four in the morning, jogs for three to five miles, then performs 2,000 sit-ups, 500 dips, 500 pushups, and 500 shrugs.

249. In Russia, giving your date a dozen roses is considered a faux pas. For happy occasions, you give an odd number of flowers while for condolences an even number.

250. In a medium McDonald's chocolate milkshake, there are 630 calories. The same calories are found in an average meal.

251. Only when a funnel cloud touches the ground is it considered a tornado.

252. In March 2017, an almost twenty six foot (eight meter) tall statue of King Samotek I, who ruled Egypt from 664 to 610 B.C, was found by a team of Egyptian and German archaeologists. Originally, it was believed to be a representation of Pharaoh Ramses II. The statue is over 3,000 years old.

253. Have you ever walked through the woods after a rain stormed and smelled a sweet lingering scent? That scent is really a bacteria called actinomycetes, and its spores are usually formed in the dry soil, until they are splashed into the air when it rains.

254. A man named Bill Haast, aka the snake man, was bitten by over one hundred snakes in his life. He injected himself with snake venom everyday for sixty years so he could build up immunity. With his antibody blood, he was able to save twenty one people who had been bitten by snakes.

255. Since the death of Steve Jobs in 2011, he has won 141 patents as of January, 2016. Out of a total of 458 patents filed by Apple, mostly related to the design of Apple products, around one-third of them were filed by Steve Jobs himself.

256. 90% of all the ice on the planet is found in Antarctica, in an area that is just under one and a half times the size of the United States. In some parts like east Antarctica, ice averages 1.2 miles (two kilometers) thick.

257. Bug Racer is a toy car powered by a live cricket. You can watch the cricket drive through a see-through windshield.

258. The male seahorse becomes pregnant instead of the female. The unfertilized eggs are passed by the female to the sperm producing male, where they are fertilized and then kept in a sealable brood pouch on the male. Ten to twenty days later, the male gives birth to thousands of babies.

259. The scents produced by flowers decrease as global temperatures increase.
260. At Super Smash Bros, poor personal hygiene and body odor were such big problems that they started to disqualify tournament participants if they stank. They went so far as to distribute deodorant to the contestants.
261. Before being elected as president, Barack Obama had won two Grammy Awards. Both were for best spoken word album: one for an audio recording of his 1995 Memoir "Dreams from My Father," and the second was for "The Audacity of Hope."
262. Dennis Morin, a fifty four year old from Quebec used a river board to swim along the Yukon River, covering 1,988 miles (3,200 kilometers) in a mere seventy five days. He swam for six hours per day on average, and he only took ten days off to rest during the whole period.
263. During the filming of The Hobbit, Sir Ian McKellen actually broke down and cried after he had to film in front of a green screen and not other actors stating: "This is not why I became an actor."
264. Napoleon Bonaparte, the French army leader, really hated losing games, particularly card games. He frequently cheated, but most people never called him out, to avoid upsetting him. His mother, however, always called him out. He in turn would tell his mother that she was rich and could afford to lose, but he was poor and needed to win.
265. In 2010, the serial killer named Rodney Alcala was his own attorney for his trial case. In a deep voice, he would interrogate himself on the witness sound addressing them to Mr. Alcala, and then answer them himself in a normal voice.
266. The longest marriage ever recorded lasted eighty six years. The North Carolina couple, named Zelmyra and Herbert Fisher, got married on May 13, 1924, and stayed together until Herbert passed away in 2011, at 105 years old.
267. Sitting on a sea turtle is considered a third degree felony in the United States.
268. In 2006, Branson, Missouri held the annual Discover Santa Convention, with workshops, vendor fairs, events, and

networking. More than 300 Santas showed up and it was the first true modern day Santa convention.

269. UPS drivers must follow a specific route that includes never turning left. Even though it can sometimes take longer to get to their destination, it reduces the chance of an accident and actually saves fuel.

270. In Collinsville, Illinois, there is a sixty nine foot (twenty one meter) tall ketchup bottle, which is the largest of the world, perched on the top of a hundred (thirty meter) foot tall steel tower. It's the water tower at the Old Brooks Ketchup Plant and Headquarters, and Collinsville holds the World's Largest Ketchup Bottle Festival every single year.

271. NASA purchased a nineteen million dollar toilet from the Space Public Corporation and SP Korolev Rocket, a Russia-based aerospace firm in 2007. The price may seem high but this toilet makes drinking water out of urine.

272. Diggerland is a kind of adventure park in England, where visitors can drive and operate real tractors, dump trucks, and other full-size construction machinery.

273. Pieces of land are being given to businesses and entrepreneurs in Dalhousie, New Brunswick, Canada. The value of the land varies from $20,000 to $50,000.

274. Sleeping under a weighted blanket seems to provide a better night's sleep to people with anxiety, depression, or insomnia. These blankets are filled with plastic pellets and add weight, and cost anywhere from $120 - $250.

275. About 45.8 pints of ice cream per year is eaten by the average US citizen, which is more than any other citizen in the world. After the United States, Australia and Norway are second and third respectively to eat the most ice cream in the world.

276. In Kansas, there is a state law that requires that all pedestrians crossing a highway at night must wear tail lights on themselves.

277. The United States spends more money on the military than the rest of the world combined. There are 8,400 attack helicopters around the globe and 6,400 of them reside in the US.

278. About three million years ago, marsupials made their way into

Australia from South America by traveling through Antarctica when it didn't have any ice.

279. When the ill-fated Donner Party set out from Springfield, Illinois, in 1846, a young lawyer named Abraham Lincoln considered joining the group on their journey. He eventually changed his mind and decided to not go given that he had a child at home and his wife Mary Todd was also pregnant.

280. Many basketball starters have donated millions of dollars to the Muhammad Ali Exhibit at the Smithsonian, some including Lebron James, Michael Jordan, and Magic Johnson.

281. To help create an underwater reef for crustaceans and fish, more than 2,500 decommissioned subway cars in New York have been dropped into the Atlantic Ocean.

282. Some of the stars that have joined the infamous "27 Club" are Jimi Hendrix, Janis Joplin, Kurt Cobain, Brian Jones from the Rolling Stones, Amy Winehouse, and Jim Morrison. They all were twenty-seven years old when they passed away.

283. The letter X is used in airport codes such as LAX in Los Angeles and PHX in Phoenix. Previously, there used to be a two-letter system, however, new standards required a three-letter identifier, so airports simply added a letter "X" to avoid changing much.

284. Rhode Island and Providence Plantations is actually the full official name of the state of Rhode Island. In 2009, the general assembly voted on whether to keep the original longer name or its shortest form. Even though they decided to keep the original name, nobody really uses it.

285. The DNA of the chicken that's served at Subway was once tested by researchers at Trent University in Ontario, Canada. The tested sample was only about 50% chicken, and the rest was soy filler.

286. In Ukraine, along the Dnieper River, one of the earliest house structures ever has been found. They are huts that date back to between 23,000 BC and 12,000 BC. They were made of mammoth bones and large pits have been found near them that contain stone tools, bone fragments, and ash.

287. FIAT workers in Sodertalje, Sweden, found out that the Google

Street View car was going to be in town, so they sent a FIAT to drive next to the car when it was going around the Volkswagen headquarters for forty five minutes.

288. In 2005, a Valentine bear called "Crazy for you Bear" was released by the Vermont Teddy Bear Company. The bear came wearing a straight jacket and commitment papers. Sales were actually good until advocates for the mentally ill protested it, and the company stopped making them.

289. In 2008, a rare event was seen over the sky where a conjunction of the Moon, Venus, and Jupiter formed a smiley face. The event was visible from all parts of the world, even in cities with light pollution like New York City.

290. 12th-century King Henry II of England had a personal entertainer named Roland the Farter. Every Christmas, he would perform a dance for the king that always ended with a jump, a fart, and a whistle at the same time. Thanks to these annual performances, he was given a manor house and over 100 acres of land.

291. In 1910, New York became the first state in America to create a law against drunk driving. It was then followed by California and eventually every other state in the country.

292. In order to save the Przewalski's horse from extinction, it was introduced to habits in the Chernobyl area. Because the area has very few if any humans in it, it turned out to be the perfect horse habitat, and the population is thriving.

293. Due to an infection, Pope Francis had one of his lungs removed when he was a teenager.

294. The cat is the only domestic animal not mentioned in the Bible.

295. The entire village of Sodeto in Spain won the lottery in 2012, except for one man who was never asked if he wanted to buy a ticket because the people selling forgot to ask him.

296. The only artist to top the charts as a solo artist, duo, trio, quartet and quintet is Paul McCartney.

297. Four year old Marina Chapman was kidnapped from her home in 1954 in Columbia, and was then abandoned in the jungle. That's where she experienced what would put a Tarzan story to

shame. Weeper capuchin monkeys took her in and raised her, and she spent the next five years sharing food, sleeping, and battling predators or rival groups of monkeys alongside her adopted wild family.

298. In 2011, a seventy five year old lady accidentally cut off the whole countries Internet in Armenia when she cut an underground cable when she was looking for copper.

299. Mugen Puti Puti was created by the Japanese in 2008, a toy made from silicon that feels like popping bubble wrap, which you can do for ever.

300. During the 2008 Olympics in Beijing, China, seahorse kebabs and deep-fried scorpion were among some of the eating options offered to visitors.

301. The first American president to have a Christmas tree in the public part of the White House was President William H. Taft. It was placed in the blue room and, in fact, the room still hosts the official Christmas tree today.

302. To help combat the cheetah's stress and focus their wild energy, zoos have begun raising puppies and cheetah kittens together.

303. Since the 1970's, Petaluma in California has been holding a world's ugliest dog contest. It's actually extremely competitive and the title is a fiercely desired one.

304. According to a study conducted in Fullerton by Iris Blandon-Gitlin, from California State University, a lie will be more convincing if peeing while telling it. There is a phenomenon called the inhibitory spillover effect where focusing on controlling your bladder also allows you to focus on hiding any signs you might have when lying.

305. In 1998, Fiona Hunter, a researcher at the University of Cambridge, and Lloyd Davis of the University of Otago were the first to report prostitution among penguins and chimpanzees. They were studying the mating patterns of the Adelie Penguins when they noticed that they prostitute themselves for things like stones or food.

306. Since 2008, singer Rihanna has had her own holiday in her home country of Barbados, which is celebrated on February

22. It's called Rihanna Day, and Prime Minister David Thompson even announced it at an awards ceremony.

307. The original floats used by Macy's during the Thanksgiving Parade were released into the air after the parade because Macy's didn't know what to do with them. The floats however, included a ticket that would fall to the ground after they popped. People who found a ticket could redeem it for a prize at the store.

308. Whenever Dwayne "The Rock" Johnson goes to a film set, he travels with his own private gym which comprises more than 39,000 pounds (18,000 kilograms) of equipment, and requires more than a hundred people to assemble.

309. Beer cans in Japan have braille on them saying that it's alcohol. Sometimes it says the manufacturer's name as well.

310. Tokyo has a hedgehog café with twenty to thirty friendly hedgehogs of different breeds that you can actually spend time with and even take home. It's the world's first café place of its type.

311. In Medieval England, before the Black Death, women were the ones who originally brewed the majority of the ale. Women in brewing are also found to date back to ancient Mesopotamia. Some of the titles given to them were alewife and brewster.

312. In Singapore there exists a floating stage above water that can hold up to 9,000 people. They use the stage for things such as concerts, soccer, and a place of celebration.

313. In Boston Harbor and Massachusetts Bay, the seawater has been found to contain tiny traces of caffeine. There are approximately 140 to 1,600 nanograms in Boston Harbor and five to seventy one nanograms in Massachusetts Bay.

314. There is a life-sized robot that looks exactly like Scarlet Johansson, constructed by product and graphic designer Ricky Ma. It took him a year and a half and cost $50,000. He named her "Mark One" and she responds to a set of programmed verbal commands spoken into a microphone.

315. According to BMC Medicine, the frequent use of saunas is related to a lower risk of death from cardiovascular disease in

men and women who are more than fifty years old. The study also showed that saunas lower blood pressure.

316. A study showed that HIV testing kits saw a 95% increase in sales after actor Charlie Sheen revealed that he was HIV positive. The study was called "The Charlie Sheen Effect."

317. The teeth of beavers contain iron, so they are capable of cutting through wood easily; this is also why they are orange-colored. Although their teeth look like they are decaying, the iron actually protects them from tooth decay.

318. Maple Taffy is a Canadian candy that's made by pouring hot maple syrup onto fresh snow. The cold from the snow quickly thickens the syrup that creates a soft candy.

319. Steven Jay Russell has escaped from prison four times. The first time, he simply walked out. Upon recapture, Russell lowered and paid his bail by pretending to be a judge, escaped his next capture by impersonating a doctor, and did so again by faking his death. He eventually received a 144 year sentence that he is still serving.

320. Pointing the sole of your feet or shoes at somebody is considered an insult in Buddhist and Muslim countries.

321. The orca that was in the movie "Free Willy," Keiko, was released back into the wild after twenty three years in captivity in 2002. Weeks after its release, it would come back to the Norwgian inlet seeking human contact and gave children rides on its back.

322. The largest mouth in the world according to the Guinness World Records belongs to the bowhead whale. It can measure up to sixteen feet (4.8 meters) long, thirteen feet (four meters) high, and eight feet (2.4 meters) wide. Its tongue alone can weigh nearly 200 pounds (ninety kilograms).

323. Oyster spat is the name given to a baby oyster.

324. Fake snow was commonly used in place of the real thing during the early days of Hollywood. Foamite, the material used in fire extinguishers, was used and mixed with sugar, water, soap flakes, corn flakes painted white, marble dust, salt and flour, and even cancer causing material asbestos.

325. The "Max Motor Dreams Cot" is a cot designed by Ford

Motors that simulates night time driving conditions, including engine noises, street lighting, and car motion. It's programmed using a smartphone app that makes it possible to record and then recreate the comforting motion, sounds, and lights from an actual journey. You can use it to put your baby to sleep without needing to take him for a drive.

326. The loudest sound ever recorded on the planet was caused by the eruption of the Krakatoa volcano in Indonesia, in 1883. It could be heard thousands of miles away in Australia and the Island of Rodriguez.

327. Given the negative effects on their textile industry, Kenya, Uganda, and Tanzania proposed a ban on the importation of second hand clothes and garments in 2015, as it put thousands of people out of work.

328. In 1905, seventy year old author Mark Twain began to collect young girls from the ages of ten to sixteen for a club, which he called "his angel fish."

329. The company "12 South" released a candle that smells like an Apple Macbook that has just been removed from the box. The company actually specializes in selling Mac accessories. The candle is made up of soy wax that is scented with mint, peach, sage, lavender, basil, and mandarin; it costs $24.

330. Bulls are actually color blind, so it doesn't really matter the color of the matador's cape. It's the motion that attracts the bull's attention to charge, not the color red.

331. Indonesia has created a male contraceptive from a plant called the gendarussa which is 99% effective.

332. Forty to fifty million years ago, Antarctica's climate was very similar to the current weather in California.

333. John Antioco, the CEO of Blockbuster, in the 1990's laughed in Reed Hastings face when he offered to form a partnership with him. That company was Netflix.

334. Twenty years ago, scientists found the bones of a Scandinavian woman that date back 5,000 years ago. When her bones and teeth were deeply examined, an ancient strain of bacteria that caused the plague was found. Scientists believe that an early

form of the plague developed in Europe between 6,100 and 5,400 years ago.

335. When a rain storm is approaching, frogs are known to croak louder. Experts think that because frogs mate and then lay eggs in bodies of freshwater, there are actually more watery places for them to choose from after a heavy rain.

336. The International Potato Center, or CIP, located in Lima, Peru, proved once that it was possible to grow potatoes on Mars, by simulating a Martian environment on Earth.

337. James Fallon, a renowned neuroscientist, studied the brains of psychopathic killers. During his studies, he scanned his own brain as a control, finding that he himself was a psychopath.

338. In Hanahan, South Carolina, there is a 4.9 feet (1.5 meter) long orange alligator living in a pond. Locals named it Trumpigator.

339. To cool wine down, ancient Egyptian pharaohs used to make slaves fan it all night.

340. One of Jennifer Lopez's nicknames in China translates to "Lord of Butt."

341. The highest bite force ever recorded was to a nineteen-foot (six meter) long Australian alligator, which has a bite force of 3,700 pounds (1,600 kilograms).

342. When nuclear weapons are detonated over high altitudes, they can cause retinal burns in the eyes if looked at without safety goggles, and the sky can light up for up to thirty minutes.

343. It's possible to get music from the classic Sega games on Spotify. Tracks like "Outrun," "Sonic the Hedgehog," "Shinobi," "Golden Axe," and "Jet Set Radio" can be found. In fact, there are more than a dozen full albums to choose from.

344. There are some countries where you can purchase beer with your meal at McDonald's, such as Germany, France, Greece, Portugal, South Korea, and Austria.

345. In a seven year study, researchers from Alberta, Canada, discovered that human urine contains at least 3,079 different chemical compounds.

346. Donald Trump once attempted to have the phrase "You're Fired" trademarked, but he was denied.

347. In 1964, Australian scientists Isabel Joy Bear and RG Thomas conducted a study to determine the reason behind that powerful, wonderful scent of fresh rain. They concluded that it's a mixture of plant oils that are secreted by some plants after an arid period, bacterial spores, and the ozone.

348. There is a new dining craze known as "Dinner in the Sky" where you actually eat your food suspended 197 feet (sixty meters) above the ground in a racing chair. It is already available in fifteen countries around the world.

349. Cognitive dysfunction syndrome is a condition similar to Alzheimer that affects dogs. It's estimated that 28% of dogs aged eleven to twelve years old suffer from this. And about 60% of dogs that are fifteen to sixteen years old also present signs of the disease.

350. Between 1969 and 1972, 841 pounds (382 kilograms) of lunar rocks, core samples, pebbles, sand, and dust from the lunar surface were brought back to Earth by six Apollo missions. The six space flights returned 2,200 separate samples from six different exploration sites on the moon.

351. Pregnancy in elephants lasts up to 680 days, the longest period known of any animal. Additionally, unlike other animals, elephants are born with an advanced level of brain development and also have a unique cycle of ovulation and hormone levels.

352. Jane Austen, the English novelist, is buried at Winchester Cathedral in England, along with the former kings that date back as far as 611 AD.

353. A Russian man named Alexei Roskov drank three bottles of vodka, jumped out of a building five stories high, walked back up, and then jumped out of it again, all because his wife was nagging at him. He survived the second time as well.

354. As a Halloween prank, a Burger King franchise in Queens, New York, covered their building with a huge, white drape, turning itself into a ghost version of a McDonald's. The marquis on the front read: "Boo! Just kidding, we still flame grill our burgers. Happy Halloween!"

355. A study conducted at the University of California Davis

revealed that adding a small amount of seaweed to a cow's diet reduces their methane production by almost 60%. This finding could lessen the amount of greenhouse gasses that bovines emit.

356. The character Gonzo, in the film "Muppets from Space," was an alien and his family came to Earth to throw a party for him. They later ask him if he could go back with them to space and even though he initially agrees, he later changes his mind to be with his Muppet friends.

357. The White House, the Treasury building, and foreign diplomatic missions in Washington along with the first family are guarded by nearly 3,200 special agents and 1,300 uniformed officers. The team also provides security to other politically relevant individuals, such as the vice president, the president-elect, the vice president-elect, former presidents and their families, presidential candidates visiting heads of state, and representatives of the US performing special missions overseas.

358. The Maya and other ancient peoples of southern North America used to go to dentists to decorate their teeth with notches, grooves, and semi-precious stones like jade.

359. The oldest working American actor today is Norman Lloyd, at 104 years old. He first appeared on screen during the Great Depression when he was just a teenager, and he has been working for eighty eight years. Originally he wanted to become a tennis champion.

360. The only four musical artists or groups who have a Billboard Top 40 single from the 1980's, 1990's, 2000's, and 2010's are Michael Jackson, Madonna, U2, and Weird Al Yankovic.

361. In the United States, 14.5% of men are over six feet tall. Despite this, 58% of CEOs at Fortune 500 Companies are more than six feet tall.

362. A seventy five pound (thirty four kilogram) natural pearl was found by a Filipino fisherman in a giant clam. He kept it hidden under his bed for ten years as a good luck charm. The pearl is 170,000 carats.

363. After collecting unwashed panties that were thrown on stage by women at his shows, musician Frank Zappa had a quilt made.

364. In London, researchers from St. George's University published a study in the Journal Archives of Disease in Childhood demonstrating that those children who spend more than three hours in front of a screen or using computers are at a greater risk of developing type II diabetes. These kids scored higher on various measures of body fat and had higher insulin levels.

365. Artificial intelligence is capable of accurately guessing if someone is gay or straight, according to a study performed at Stanford University, in 2017. Researches created a computer algorithm that could distinguish between gay and straight men 81% of the time, while for women it was 74% of the time.

366. For gorillas, burping is something they do when they feel happy and at ease.

367. The most people that can fit into a classic model Mini according to the Guinness World Records is twenty seven. It was achieved on May 18, 2014, by Dani and the Miniskirts in Brighton, England.

368. In 1945, during President Andrew Jackson's funeral, his pet parrot was kicked out for cursing.

369. Nintendo 64 wasn't always known by that name. It was first called Project Reality, then later renamed to Nintendo Ultra 64, until the name was finally shortened to Nintendo 64.

370. The St. Malo castle walls in France are notorious for being a safe haven for pirates.

371. Ukulele is the word for a music instrument, and in Hawaii where it originates, it loosely translates to "jumping flea." It's named that because the movements that a person's fingers make when playing the instrument resemble those of a quick hopping insect.

372. In 2004, in Chicago, a bus that was transporting the Dave Matthews Band dumped 797 pounds (362 kilograms) of waste off a bridge into a river, splashing onto a boat full of tourists. The driver was sentenced to eighteen months of probation, 150 hours of community service, and $10,000 in fines.

373. Despite having DNA evidence of the suspect, German police

could not prosecute a 6.8 million dollar jewel heist because the DNA belonged to identical twins; police could not prove to whom the DNA belonged to.

374. The creator of Doritos, Arch West, was buried with his creation sprinkled over his body.

375. Frogs cannot swallow keeping their eyes open.

376. A totally waterproof MP3 player was released by Sony in 2013. They sold each one fully submerged in a water bottle in order to prove the underwater capabilities of the device.

377. Between 1347 and 1350, approximately twenty million people were killed in Europe by the Bubonic Plague, also known as Black Death. That was close to the 30% of the continent's population at the time.

378. At the Dearborn Days Community Festival in Michigan, on August 13, 1941, Henry Ford presented a new car. It was called the soybean car because it was partly made of soybean, and it only weighed two thirds of what a standard steel car did.

379. Eructation is the proper medical term for burping or belching.

380. In 2001, actor Russell Crowe was informed by the FBI that the Al-Qaeda terrorist group was planning to kidnap him as part of a cultural destabilization plot. During the filming of his movies "A Beautiful Mind" and "Master and Commander: The Far Side of the World," he required extra security; in fact, he was followed around by the FBI for almost two years.

381. Parthenophobia is a type of social anxiety where sufferers have an abnormal and persistent fear of young girls, specifically virgins.

382. An analysis of hundreds of basketball halftime speeches from several high school and college games was performed by the Journal of Applied Psychology. The result showed that the more negative the coach was at halftime, the better the team played in the second half, even if a team was already up at half-time.

383. Singer Johnny Cash received death threats from the KKK. The group saw a picture of him with his first wife and thought she was black; she was actually an Italian American woman.

384. The reason why t-shirts are called that are because they are shaped like a "T" when laid down.

385. An adult gray wolf can eat more than twenty two pounds (ten kilograms) of meat in only one sitting.

386. In Korea, there is a culture called fan death, which means that a running electric fan in a closed room with unopened windows will be fatal. Although there is no evidence to support this belief, Korean people do believe it.

387. Some of the Apollo 11 astronauts are on the Hollywood walk of fame such as Neil Armstrong, Edwin E. Buzz Aldrin Jr., and Michael Collins. Their marker isn't in the shape of a star, but round like the Moon.

388. Since 1982, Clinton Montana has hosted a five day long festival called the Montana Testicle Festival, and the main event involves competitors eating bull testicles.

389. The moons of the moon are called "sub moons," according to astronomers Una Cormaya of the Carnegie Institute for Science and Shawn Raymond of the Laboratory du Astophysice du Bordeaux. Other scientists, however, are using the term "moon moons." There are no known moon moons in our solar systems.

390. In 1998, a professor of cybernetics at Reading University named Kevin Warwick became the first technical cyborg of the world. He had a radio frequency ID implanted in his arm and could turn on the lights by snapping his fingers.

391. In 1999, the company "Excite" turned down the offer to buy Google for one million dollars. Even when Google reduced the price to $750,000, they still rejected the offer. Today Google's market cap stands at $320 billion.

392. According to a study led by researchers from The University of Queensland and Monash University, the protein found in funnel-web spider venom may protect the human brain from damage after suffering a stroke. The venom was recreated in a lab and it was found that the protein blocked acid-sensing ion channels in the brain, which is one of the key things that cause brain damage after a stroke.

393. There is actually a difference between terror and horror. Terror

occurs in anticipation of the horrifying experience, while horror occurs after.

394. The most credentialed person in history is Michael Nicholson, from Michigan. He has one bachelor degree, two associate degrees, twenty two master degrees, three specialist degrees, and one doctoral degree.

395. In 1994, Leonardo da Vinci's Codex Leicester notebook was bought by Bill Gates for $30.8 million. Besides adding the item to his personal collection, he used it to also help promote Windows Vista's launch, by using a program called Turning the Pages 2.0 that would let people browse through virtual versions of the notebook.

396. "Hikikomori" is a kind of condition suffered by around a million people in Japan, mostly men, who have locked themselves in their bedrooms for years, resulting in social and health problems.

397. In 2014, an entire family died from the fumes of rotting potatoes in their cellar, except for an eight year old girl. Each family member checked on the other by walking into the cellar, but died instantly as soon as they entered the room.

398. Students in North Korea have textbooks that claim their leader Kim Jong-Un learned to drive when he was only three years old.

399. In Iceland, a highway construction project was stopped in 2014 because some people protested the potential destruction of a church that's only attended by elves, which was along the path of the construction. The city actually had to facilitate the church, which only appears as a gigantic boulder to the naked human eye, to be safely moved out of the way with a crane, before the construction could go on.

400. According to a study published by a research team from the University of Florida, bed bugs love the colors black and red, and hate yellow and green.

401. Winston Churchill drinking habits were a bit questionable. He used to have three to four weak whiskey sodas, a bottle of wine or champagne with lunch, and another with dinner, and finished off with either cognac or brandy.

402. Thirty eight year old Shen Sing Sung was at home in High Bay province, China, when, on October 29, 2012, thirty to fifty thugs showed up and attacked him on the orders of a property developer who wanted his land. Shen was a Kung Fu expert, and as the thugs forced their way into his house, he bravely fought them off and knocked a few of them unconscious. He succeeded in defending his home as the rest of the thugs retreated.

403. Giovanni Giacomo Cassanova, or better known as just Cassanova, was actually preparing to become a priest when he discovered his vocation as a lover and libertine.

404. In 1973, a computer at MIT predicted that by the year 2040 our society would end as a result of overpopulation, pollution levels, or lack of natural resources on Earth.

405. On April 14, 1986, the biggest hailstones ever recorded hit Bangladesh. They weighed over two pounds (one kilogram) each and killed ninety two people.

406. During the London 2012 Olympic Games, a specially designed radio-controlled Mini was used to transport javelins, hammers, shots, and discusses around the field. The mini Minis were thirty nine inches (ninety nine centimeters) long and could carry loads of up to forty pounds (eighteen kilograms).

407. Named after RnB singer Luther Vandross, the Luther Burger is made of a Krispy Kreme donut with bacon and cheese. It's rumored that the singer invented the burger himself when he was short on hamburger buns.

408. Nightclub owner Ruth Ellis was the last woman to be executed for murder in Great Britain, on July 13, 1955. She was hanged for killing her boyfriend. The death penalty for murder was actually banned in England, Scotland, and Wales in 1965.

409. A yoctosecond is one-trillionth of a trillionth of a second. It is comparable to the time that it takes light to cross an atomic nucleus.

410. When the secretary of Steve Jobs was once late to work, Steve handed her the keys to his Jaguar and said "don't be late again."

411. Yao Ming, the retired NBA All-Star basketball player, has his

own winery in Napa Valley. It opened in 2009 as Yao Family Wines; they make ultra-premium wines and it's open from ten to five for tastings.

412. In the spring of 2017, facial recognition technology began being used by the Canadian Border Services Agency at major Canadian airports. To keep out alleged terrorists and other criminals, the technology compares images of people arriving in the country with photographs of suspects on watch lists.

413. In 2015, a study done by Common Sense Media and CEO James Steyer revealed that the average teen spends up to nine hours a day on social media.

414. Dr. Rush's Bilious Pill was a type of remedy taken by the explorers of the Lewis and Clark when they felt constipated on their journey. The pill was made of ten grains of calomel which contains mercury. Experts were able to locate the exact spot where they camped in Montana by finding some signatures of mercury in their pit latrines. Before they set off on their journey, Lewis and Clark were informed by American President Thomas Jefferson that they would possibly encounter mountains of salt, Welsh speaking Indians, herds of wooly mammoths and giant ground sloths. Although they did not encounter any of these things, Lewis did find 178 species of plants that were unknown, as well as 122 new animals such as grizzly bears and coyotes.

415. In 2001, a boy named Jessie Arbogast was attacked by a seven foot (2.1 meter) bull shark. His uncle not only saved Jesse from the shark, but he also dived back in, seized the shark, and wrestled it to shore where a ranger shot it, so they could retrieve the severed arm of his nephew. The arm was pried from its gullet and was placed on ice, then rushed to the hospital. Incredibly, it was sewed back on successfully.

416. Don Gorski, a sixty four year old man from Wisconsin, ate the 30,000th Big Mac of his life on May 4, 2018. Don holds the world record for being the single person who's consumed the highest number of Big Macs, and according to him, the sandwiches make up ninety to 95% of the food he eats daily.

417. Igor Vorozhbitsyn, a forty two year old Russian fisherman,

was violently being attacked by a bear when suddenly Justin Bieber's Baby ringtone went off from his phone, scaring the bear away into the woods. The ringtone had been installed by his granddaughter on his phone and it literally saved his life.

418. Being clean-shaven became popular in the US after the troops returned home as heroes from World War I. Soldiers had been required to shave so that gas masks could securely fit on their face.

419. Adolf Hitler gave a methamphetamine-based pill called pervitin to German soldiers. It was marketed as a pickup pill that supposedly reduced stress and fatigue, and brought on euphoria.

420. The domain name VacationRentals.com was bought for a whopping $35 million.

421. Cat owners have been known to compare their cat's head to the smell of sunshine or freshly baked bread. After spending four months sniffing cats, a company in Japan actually made a spray that makes everything smell like a cat's head.

422. The Incas used to measure their units of time based on the time a potato would take to be cooked.

423. It's possible for tonsils and adenoids to grow back after surgery, although it's not very common. If even a small amount of tissue is left behind, the whole thing can grow back.

424. A person who totally abstains from consuming alcohol is called a "teetotaler." To teetotal literally means to never consume alcohol.

425. Famous NBA superstars Stephen Curry, of the Golden State Warriors, and LeBron James, of the Los Angeles Lakers, were both born in Akron, Ohio.

426. Sperm whale oil was often used by the automotive industry to lubricate new cars years ago. In fact, the substance was so good that huge mammals were actually hunted almost to extinction. As a result, the US declared sperm whales an endangered species and switched to the new whale-free automatic transmission fluid.

427. The dwarf crocodile is the smallest crocodile in the world. It

measures about 5.5 feet (1.7 meters) in length and weighs only thirteen pounds (six kilograms).

428. Because boxer Muhammad Ali didn't want the name of Muhammad to be stepped on, his star on the Walk of Fame was actually placed on the wall.

429. In 1948, the Chicago Daily Tribune mistakenly announced that Thomas Dewey had won the US presidential election race when it was actually Harry S. Truman who won.

430. The tomb of the poet and writer Oscar Wilde in Paris, France, is covered in thousands of lipstick kiss marks left by years of female fans who have visited his grave.

431. According to astronomers' calculations, it takes the sun 226 million years to completely orbit around the center of the Milky Way Galaxy. Since the sun was formed 4.6 billion years ago, it has completed this orbit only 20.4 times. The last time it did it, dinosaurs roamed the Earth.

432. The Japanese term "tsundoku" refers to the act of getting reading materials or books and piling them up at home without ever reading them.

433. In New York, when the Rockefeller Center Christmas tree is taken down each year, it's used as lumber for Habitat for Humanity, a non-profit charity.

434. The singer of "Ex's and Oh's," Elle King, is actor Rob Schneider's daughter.

435. In Japan, it's possible to buy a fan just for your armpits. The cooling device was developed by gadget-maker named "Thanko." It's a small fan that clips onto your sleeve to deliver cool air to your armpits for five to nine hours. Although it's a battery-run device, you can also connect it to your PC or a battery pack.

436. After the death of Meow in 2012, a cat who weighed forty pounds (eighteen kilograms), the Guinness Book of World Records no longer records the heaviest pets in the world to discourage intentional overeating.

437. Scientists have trained some African giant pouched rats to detect tuberculosis using their sense of smell, and they've been found to be more accurate that most lab tests.

46

438. The Chinese population's demand for surgical masks has increased due to the bad air pollution. They have even become a fashion statement with designer brands coming out with their own masks.

439. A man in China once spent forty thousand dollars in 2014 to buy out all the seats in two IMAX theaters because an ex-girlfriend from seven years earlier dumped him for not being able to afford movie tickets.

440. The world record for the longest distance pulled by a horse while fully engulfed in flames is held by Joseph Toedtling, from Austria. He traveled 0.3 miles (half a kilometer) completely on fire on June 27, 2015.

441. New Zealand has two official national anthems of equal importance. One is "God Defends New Zealand" and the other is "God Save the Queen." The latter has been New Zealand's official anthem all the way back to 1840, but it's rarely sung in the country.

442. A professor from the University of Syracuse invented a multi-colored tree that produces over forty types of different fruits. The name of the tree is "The Tree of Forty Fruit."

443. When filming Django Unchained, actor Leonardo DiCaprio, who plays Calvin Candie, smashes his hand on a dinner table and accidentally crushes a stemmed glass with his palm. His hand started to bleed, but the actor finished the scene and gave an amazing performance. Director Quentin Tarantino decided to include the scene in the movie.

444. Alex Stone, an American high school student from South Carolina, was arrested and suspended from school due to a creative writing assignment where he mentioned buying a gun to shoot his neighbor's pet dinosaur.

445. For a short period of time during 1913, it was legal to mail your baby. The only condition was that the baby had to meet the eleven pound (five kilograms) weight limit. This showed just how much rural communities trusted postal workers then.

446. By communicating with the brain, Gut Microbiota can make changes in one's mood or personality.

447. Blowing smoke in someone's face can be considered a case of assault and battery in the US.

448. The world's largest model railroad is Northlandz in Flemington, New Jersey. It has over eight miles (thirteen kilometers) of track and lifelike scenery, with 3,000 tiny buildings, and over thirty nine feet (twelve meters) of bridges. It has 100 trains, 400 bridges, and over 500,000 tiny trees.

449. In the early 1900's, celery was a popular delicacy among many Americans. Restaurants would offer it in many different ways, such as mashed celery, fried celery, and celery tea. Kalamazoo, Michigan, was also known as the celery capital of the world.

450. There were so many murders between the 1970's and 1980's in Miami that the Medical Examiners had to rent refrigerated trailers from Burger King to fit all the extra corpses they had coming in.

451. According to records, the last time that all the planets in the solar system were aligned was 561 BC. The next alignment will take place in 2854.

452. Back in the 1930's, mothers and nannies used to put babies inside newly invented baby cages, and then left them outside the window so they could get fresh air.

453. In several places, drinking alcohol is prohibited before firearm shooting competitions because alcohol is regarded as a performance enhancing drug in that sport. Drinking calms the nerves, so it can literally steady the hands of a competitive shooter.

454. Sweat is actually odorless. But when bacteria on the skin and hair metabolize the proteins and fatty acids in sweat, the unpleasant odor is then produced.

455. Some buildings in the US, such as the White House, the Empire State Building, the Sears Building, and the Dodger Stadium, are so large that they have their own zip codes.

456. In Bolivia, there is a limestone wall that has over 5,000 dinosaur footprints, some of them dating back nearly sixty eight million years.

457. The most photographed person from the 1800's is American abolitionist Frederick Douglass.

458. 50,000 people signed a 2015 petition to drop the name Australian Dollar, and to adopt "Dollarydoo" as the official name of Australia's currency. The term Dollarydoo originates from an episode of the Simpsons.

459. Originally Play-Doh was manufactured as a product to clean coal residue from wallpaper.

460. Lawyers were actually banned from the state of Georgia from 1733 to 1755. In fact, they were considered pests and the scourge of mankind. At the time, it was believed that every person was perfectly capable of pleading their own case when required.

461. According to studies, if you're feeling sad, drawing a picture of your favorite food can actually cheer you up. In 2013, a study by researchers at St. Bonaventure University in New York showed that people who drew pictures of pizza and cupcakes had up to a 28% increase in their moods.

462. The last flight of the Concorde jet was in 2003. It could fly at a maximum speed of 1,350 miles (2,100 kilometers) per hour. It could go from London to New York City in about three hours, which was about half the time of other passenger planes.

463. Dexter Holland, the lead singer of the famous punk band The Offspring, is also a molecular biologist. He attended the University of Southern California where he received his master's degree. In fact, he had to withdraw from his Ph.D. program candidature due to the success of the band.

464. Ninety five year old actress Betty White holds the Guinness record for the longest TV career for a female entertainer, starting her career back in the 1950's.

465. In 1936, the founder of Adidas drove to the Olympics and persuaded US sprinter Jessie Owens to wear his shoes. As Owens successfully won four medals, letters came in from other national teams interested in buying their shoes. By World War II, they were selling 200,000 pairs a year.

466. In June 1959, 3,000 letters on the Postal Service were mailed by the US Navy via a guided missile, which was fired towards an air station in Mayport, Florida. The attempt was successful and reached the station in twenty two minutes.

49

467. Research conducted in 1978 followed over five hundred people who were prevented from attempting suicide found that, thirty years later, 90% were still alive or had died from natural causes. The study concluded that suicidal behaviors are impulsive and spur of the moment, that can be prevented.

468. Ferret-legging used to be a sport in the past, where a ferret was strapped in a contestant's pants, without wearing any underwear. The competitor who could stand the teeth and claws the longest would win.

469. More than 70% of all rail journeys in the United Kingdom either start or finish in London.

470. The Meganeuropsis is the largest known insect of all-time. It looks like a dragonfly and measures roughly fifteen inches (forty seven centimeters) long with a wingspan of thirty inches (seventy five centimeters) long.

471. On the Titanic, there were over thirteen couples celebrating their honeymoon. Unfortunately, none of them survived upon impact and the subsequent sinking of the boat.

472. The first-ever toy advertised on TV was Mr. Potato Head, back in 1952. Almost two million were sold in the first year alone.

473. Actor from the hit television show "The Office," Rainn Wilson, had a pet sloth while he was growing up.

474. Some women have a rare trait which gives them four color receptor cells in their eyes letting them see up to one hundred million colors. The average human only has three color receptors which let them see about a million colors.

475. The Andromeda galaxy is so gigantic that if it were brighter and we could see it, it would look bigger than the moon to us. To put it into perspective, the moon is at a distance of 248,400 miles (400,000 kilometers) from Earth, but the Andromeda galaxy is fifteen quintillion miles (twenty five quintillion kilometers), or 2.5 million light years away from us.

476. Ten years after the 9/11 events, the New York Times created a "Portraits of Grief" which was an archive of articles about all the victims of 9/11 and how the families are coping with the grief.

477. The New Testament has been translated into 1,534 different

languages. In fact, it's currently in the process of being translated into some 2,659 more languages.

478. In a single stride, ostriches' long legs can cover nine to sixteen feet (three to five meters). Their legs can also act as powerful weapons. One kick for example can kill a human or a potential predator like a lion.

479. In June 2016, a study performed by researchers from the Yale University of Public Health determined that people who read books live an average of two years longer than those who don't.

480. Located in Denver, the Denver International Airport is over twice the size of the whole Manhattan Island. It's America's largest airport, and is home to the biggest jet fuel distribution network on Earth.

481. Currently, Michael Jordan makes more money each year than he earned in salary during his fifteen year NBA career.

482. Microsoft lowered their flags to half-staff when Apple's founder Steve Jobs died in 2011, as a sign of respect to him.

483. On July 23, 1983, Air Canada's Flight 143 with sixty nine people on board ran out of fuel at an altitude of seven miles (twelve kilometers). Incredibly, the highly experienced pilot managed to glide the plane down safely and land it without anyone getting hurt.

484. Germans consume the highest volume of candy per capita in the world, with each person eating twenty eight pounds (thirteen kilograms) of sugar, chocolate and gum candy on average.

485. According to the annual statistics of the American Cancer Society, the death rate from cancer in the United States has gradually declined over the past two decades, falling 23% from its peak in 1991 all the way up to 2012. This translates to about 1.7 million deaths averted.

486. The Australian Bull Oak is known to be the hardest wood in the world; it requires 5,060 pounds (2,295 kilograms) of force to embed a steel ball into it. On the contrary, the softest wood in the world is the Cuipo, which only requires around twenty two pounds (ten kilograms) of force to embed a steel ball inside of it.

487. It is illegal to commit suicide in Japan by jumping in front of a train or killing yourself in your apartment building. The building or train company can sue the family for clean up fees, income loss and any negative publicity that might be brought upon by the suicide.

488. US Navy torpedo motors used 180 proof grain alcohol as fuel in the Second World War, and naval officers often stole the fuel and added pineapple juice to make an alcoholic beverage they called torpedo juice. The authorities started mixing poisonous chemicals into the fuel to discourage this practice, but the ingenious sailors always figured out ways to remove the poison from the alcohol.

489. Phyllis Penzo had a humble job waiting tables in Yonkers, New York at Sal's Pizzeria, when in April, 1984, a customer asked her to pick numbers for a lottery ticket. Robert Cunningham, the customer in question, ended up winning a six million dollar prize, and the gentleman that he was, he split the prize with Penzo, giving her three million dollars.

490. After the First World War, much of the battlefield was barren and the red poppy was among the few plants that grew on the land, which is why it became the remembrance symbol that's been worn for decades.

491. The term freelancer comes from the medieval era, when warriors were not under the oath of any lord, hence making them a freelance.

492. There are differences among jam, jelly, marmalade, and preserves. Jam is a thick mixture of fruit, pectin, and sugar that's boiled rapidly until the fruit is soft, but thick enough to spread easily. Jelly is different in that it's made from sugar, pectin, acid, and fruit juice that turn into a clear spread. Marmalade is a spread made from the peel and pulp of citrus fruit which is cooked for a long time. And finally, preserves are chunks of fruit that are surrounded by jelly.

493. When NBA superstar Michael Jordan was at high school, he was actually cut from his Laney High School varsity basketball team.

494. Independent Studio Services makes a prop beer that is used in

several movies and television shows. It's called Heisler Beer or Heisler Gold Ale, and it has appeared on "Beerfest," "Brooklyn Nine-Nine," and "Parks and Recreation."

495. In the presidential election of 1872, women's rights activist Susan B. Anthony voted illegally. She was tried, convicted, and sentenced to pay a $100 fine. Although she didn't pay it, she was released anyway.

496. The generic term used for various small fish that are sealed in cans or other containers is sardine.

497. Two years after being retired, 78% of all former NFL players become bankrupt or under financial stress. For NBA players, 60% of them are broke within five years of retirement.

498. There is a mobile game called "Send Me to Heaven" that consists of throwing your phone as high as you can in the air. The inventor made it with the aim of destroying as many iPhones as possible, but Apple immediately banned it from the app store.

499. James Buchanan, the 15th President of the United States, used to buy slaves with his own money in order to free them.

500. A woman once took part in a search for a missing tourist in Iceland. Hours later she realized she was the missing person everyone was searching for.

501. In 1252, the King of Norway gave a polar bear to King Henry III. It was kept in the Tower of London chained up with a collar around its neck. Despite this, the animal was allowed to swim and hunt for fish in the River Thames.

502. Around two billion people in the world eat insects as part of their everyday diet. They are known to contain high amounts of protein and are usually inexpensive. The only region where they are not consumed is in the West.

503. Studies show that most missing children are actually abducted by parents or relatives.

504. Armand Hammer, a businessman, coincidentally served as a director for the company Arm and Hammer.

505. "Need A Mom" is the name of a business established by entrepreneur Nina Keneally in Brooklyn, New York. The

service involves renting a mom for forty dollars, who will listen to you, give you advice, cook, and help you with chores.

506. There is a type of bird called "potoos" that use body posture to camouflage themselves in nature looking like the part of a tree stump.

507. Someone who works with iron and steel is called a blacksmith, while someone who works with white metal such as tin and pewter is called a whitesmith. There is also a brownsmith who works with brass and copper.

508. In 2007, actor Daniel Radcliffe, famous for his role as Harry Potter, wore exactly the same clothes in London for six months in a row so that paparazzi would end up with the same photos every day, thus not being able to publish the pictures.

509. As of 2016, there are about 35,402 people living with HIV in Atlanta, Georgia, according to AIDSVu. The majority of them are men.

510. A two and a half year old boy named Michelle Funk fell into a creek near her home in Salt Lake City on June 10, 1986. She was rescued an hour later, but she had no pulse and wasn't breathing. Doctors put her on a heart lung bypass machine and rewarmed her blood. Amazingly, when her blood finally warmed to seventy-seven degrees Fahrenheit (twenty five degrees Celsius), she woke up and is still living to this day.

511. Up to five million people worldwide are bitten by snakes every year according to the World Health Organization. The majority of these events occur in Africa and Southeast Asia.

512. In 2014, the earliest evidence of human footprints was discovered by scientists outside of Africa, on the Norfolk coast in the east of England. The footprints were found on the shores of Happisburgh and were more than 800,000 years old.

513. Located in Newark, New Jersey, the world's largest indoor farm is 21,024 square feet (6,410 square meter). These types of farms can grow crops without soil, sunlight, and nearly no water. In fact, they use 95% less water than conventional outdoor farms.

514. In 1989, on April Fool's Day, Richard Branson created a hot air

balloon to look like a UFO and hired a dwarf to wear an ET costume and scare anyone who came near it.

515. In 2016, the Journal of Evolutionary Biology published a study suggesting that when it comes to facial hair on men, more women prefer them to have five to ten days of growth instead of being clean-shaven.

516. The corpse flower is a type of flower that only blooms every seven to ten years. The flower actually smells like putrefying and decaying flesh.

517. The proportion of the world's population over sixty years old, according to the World Health Organization, will nearly double from 12% to 22% between 2015 and 2050. In addition, about 80% of those older people will be living in low and middle income countries.

518. The belief that balding comes from the mother's side of the family is actually a myth according to Men's Journal. In fact, it comes from the genes from both sides of the family. It's also a myth that wearing hats will make you go bald.

519. Theoretically, it's possible to get addicted to cuddling. Couples that tend to cuddle a lot can experience oxytocin withdrawal when they are not together.

520. Former President Richard Nixon was able to play five instruments: the piano, the saxophone, the clarinet, the accordion, and the violin.

521. The Otton frog is a rare Japanese frog species that carries a hidden weapon. They have retractable claws that can shoot out from their thumbs. They use these claws as switchblades to fight and mate.

522. There is no way to hum if your nose is completely plugged.

523. Every twenty seven days, your human skin regenerates itself. The skin replaces itself 900 times on average in one lifetime. Tattoos are however not replaced when the skin regenerates because the ink is infused deep inside the dermis layer, so it doesn't fall away or get exfoliated, and may only come off if you are injured.

524. Florida has a mythical creature called the "Skunk Ape," the same way that Northern States have the legend of BigFoot. It's

said to be a 7.87 feet (2.4 meter) tall human-like primate, and it smells like cow manure or rotten eggs, according to stories that were very popular in the 1970's. There were so many reported sightings of this creature that state lawmakers even tried to make it a criminal misdemeanor to kidnap, possess, molest, or hurt humanoid or anthropoid animals.

525. Since 1954, more Burger King fast-food places have burned down than any other fast food chain.

526. In 2017, a rule against putting the number 69 on drivers' license plates was issued by the California Department of Motor Vehicles, except if the year model of the vehicle is 1969.

527. No two wolves will howl on the same note when howling together. Instead, they harmonize to create the illusion that there are more wolves than there actually are.

528. "Shewee" is a portable urination device that allows women and girls to urinate while standing and without removing any clothes.

529. The "Royal March" is Spain's national anthem. It has no lyrics.

530. The three wise monkeys actually have names. The see no evil monkey is named Mizaru, the hear no evil monkey is named Mikazaru, and the speak no evil monkey is named Mazaru.

531. Levi Mayhew was a terminally ill six year old boy who gave up his own Make-A-Wish Foundation gift, by giving it to a little girl who was writing Levi letters of encouragement. She went to Florida with a cutout photo of Levi on all the rides.

532. When Chrissy Metz was cast as Kate on the show "This Is Us," her contract obliged her to progressively lose weight over the span of the show. She accepted those terms, and many fans have been inspired to take the journey with her, towards a healthier self.

533. Photographer Andrew Suryono was under heavy rain when he noticed an orangutan using a leaf for shelter. He quickly took the shot that made him earn an honorable mention in the 2015 National Geographic photo contest.

534. According to a 2010 report, it's estimated that about 30,000 elephants a year are killed by poachers to keep up with the global demand for ivory. As a result, the United States has

adopted a near-total ivory ban since July, 2016. In fact, the previous year, more than a ton of ivory was crushed in New York City as part of the US government's effort to crack down on the illegal trade.

535. If you want to speed up the ripening process of green tomatoes, you can place them with a ripe banana or apple in an enclosed space. Furthermore, there is a gas called ethylene that helps speed up ripening, which is used commercially with tomatoes and other fruits that are picked green before shipping and then ripened for sale.

536. Dementia Village, a small village in Holland, is inhabited by people with dementia. The village has been designed to be a normal environment with grocery stores, restaurants, cafes, and gardens, within a secure perimeter. Patients can safely roam around without feeling locked down or confused.

537. There is a form of art called non visible art. The works are imagined by an artist then described to an audience. A woman named Amie Davidson bought a piece in 2011 for ten thousand dollars stating that she "really identified with the ideology of the non visible art project."

538. About fifty ounces (1.5 liters) of clear and thin phlegm are created by a healthy person's sinuses a day, and most of it is swallowed.

539. American presidents are not allowed to go to the top of the Gateway Arch in St. Louis, Missouri, as the US Secret Service forbids it. The only one who was the exception to this rule was Dwight D. Eisenhower, when he visited the monument in 1967 at seventy seven years old. The Arch was actually closed to the public as he insisted on riding the tram to the top.

540. A man named Walter Orthmann from Brazil holds the Guinness World Record for the longest career with one company. He started working for Industrias Renaux S.A. back in 1938 and continues to work for the company, which is now called "RenauxView," as of April 2, 2018.

541. Scientists discovered an abandoned termite mound in the Miombo Woodland area of Central Africa that is thought to be more than 2,200 years old.

542. On June 7, 2017, in the Swedish city of Helsingborg, the Museum of Failure was opened for the first time. It was purposefully created by Samuel West who wanted people to think differently about failure by realizing that success wouldn't exist without it.

543. Whenever actor Kevin Bacon is invited to a wedding, he always bribes the DJ not to play the song "Footloose." The reason behind is that he does not want to upstage the bride and groom on their big day.

544. According to William A. Hiscock from Montana State University, if you were in a spaceship that continually accelerated at 1G and traveled to the center of our galaxy and back, it would only take forty years. However, after coming back, 60,000 years will have passed on Earth although only forty years have passed for you. This means that you can technically go into the future.

545. The giant hogweed is federally listed as a dangerous and noxious plant. Contact with its sap can cause the skin to be extremely sensitive to sunlight.

546. The fastest shark in the world is the mako shark. It can swim as fast as sixty miles (ninety six kilometers) per hour, while the average shark only swims at a speed of 1.5 miles (2.4 kilometers) per hour.

547. People in love can simultaneously match their heartbeats simply by gazing into one another's eyes.

548. In February 2017, a survey based on Venezuela's living conditions showed that almost 75% of the population lost an average of at least 18.9 pounds (8.6 kilograms) in 2016, due to a lack of proper nutrition because of the economic crisis.

549. The military channel voiceover for the 2005 video game "Call of Duty 2: The Big Red One" was done by actor Mark Hamill.

550. Mosquitoes use a Zen-like approach of non-resistance in order to survive the impact of raindrops.

551. Beach Boys drummer Mike Love is the uncle of NBA all-star Kevin Love of the Cleveland Cavaliers.

552. Amazonian butterflies have been known to drink turtle tears so they can receive mineral sodium from them.

553. The oldest joke in recorded history, according to the University of WolverHampton, dates back to 1900 B.C., in ancient Sumeria. The joke essentially stated: Here's something that has never happened from the beginning of time; a young wife farting in her husband's lap.

554. Kinder Surprise, the candy-filled eggs made by Italian company Ferrero, are actually illegal in the United States. According to the US Food, Drug and Cosmetic Act, all candies embedded with non-nutri-shiv objects are banned in the country. If you bring these candies into the United States, you can be fined up to $1,200 per egg.

555. Astronaut ice cream has always been a myth according to Vox, as it has never been eaten in space. In fact, it was used as a marketing ploy to influence the young and impressionable ones.

556. Back in 1903, a man named John Thurman started a horse-drawn vacuum system offering a door-to-door service. It cost $4 per home.

557. Andre the Giant left home at the age of fourteen years old to find work. When he returned home at nineteen, he had grown so much that his parents didn't recognize him. They did recognize him from wrestling on television, but they did not know that he was their son.

558. In 1979, the residents of Naco, Arizona, and Mexico, had a volleyball match over the fence of the border that divides them. From then on, it has become an annual tradition.

559. A small bird called an Arctic tern was spotted in 2016, migrating from the English coast to Antarctica, and then flying back again. It flew 59,000 miles (96,000 kilometers) in total, which turned out to be the longest recorded migration. That's the same as flying around the Earth's circumference twice, and then adding another 9,900 miles (16,000 kilometers).

560. There are no muscles in our fingers to facilitate movement. Flexing and curling our fingers, for example, is actually made possible by specific actions of the tendons, bones, and muscles that are found in the palm of our hands.

561. In 1881, in Tombstone, Arizona, the famous gunfight that took

place at the OK Corral between the Earp Brothers along with Doc Holiday against the cowboys lasted only thirty seconds.

562. Expiration dates for bottled water actually applies for the bottle, not for the water itself.

563. While in water, fish can actually drown or suffocate. They get their oxygen directly from the water through their gills so if for some reason that water runs out of oxygen, they drown just like an air-breathing animal would.

564. To attract females, male capuchin monkeys urinate on their hands and cover their body with urine.

565. In Peru, vultures are equipped with GoPros and GPS trackers to help find illegal trash dumps.

566. Cheetos Burrito was a new product released by Taco Bell in August of 2016. It was a burrito stuffed with seasoned meat, buttery rice and a cheese sauce and Cheetos that cost just a dollar.

567. In the United States, around 795,000 people have a stroke every year with about three in four being first time strokes. In fact, every forty seconds, someone in the United States has a stroke.

568. "The Boss" is a big grizzly bear that lives in Bath, Canada. According to residents, he has eaten two black bears; he walks through the town in the middle of the day and has fathered many of the bears that live in Banff, Yoho, and Kootenay National Parks.

569. In the 1700's you could come into the Zoo of London for free if you brought a dog or cat to feed the lions.

570. Paradoxical undressing occurs when people are experiencing hypothermia and, suddenly, they feel irrationally hot and want to take off their clothes.

571. If you were to double a penny every day, after thirty days you'd have five million dollars.

572. Due to an unintended acceleration in Toyota vehicles, once the company had to recall over nine million of their cars and had to pay more than $3 billion in fines and settlements.

573. The planet Saturn is mostly made up of gas. If it was put in a really large bathtub, it would float.

574. In 2015, Japan finally lifted its sixty seven year old ban on dancing that ruled after World War II. They prohibited dancing in venues without a special dance license. Originally the law intended to crack down on dance halls that were often a hotbed for prostitution.

575. There is a neuropathic disorder called trigeminal neuralgia that causes episodes of intense pain in the face that comes from the trigeminal nerve. The pain is so intense and excruciating that the disorder is referred to as suicide disease.

576. Endling is the name given to the last individual of a single species. When it dies, the species is extinct for good.

577. 1% of static on your television comes from the light of the Big Bang.

578. On August 21, 1986, a volcanic lake known as Lake Nyos in Cameroon, Africa, released 1.2 cubic kilometers of CO_2 in approximately twenty seconds, suffocating over 1,746 people. This massive wave of deadly gas swept over the countryside, killing people as far away as fifteen miles (twenty five kilometers).

579. There is a perfume that is Play-Doh-scented.

580. In 1922, a referendum to ban alcohol took place in Sweden, but it failed with 51% of the voters choosing against it. The decision was split between the sexes with 63% of women voting for the prohibition and 63% of men voting against it.

581. "FrankenStrat" is a guitar created by musician Eddie Van Halen, combining different parts of the instrument from various places. This was his attempt to have the classical sound of a Gibson mixed with the physical attributes of the Fender.

582. Exercising is not only good for you but increases your productivity. Regularly exercising makes you smarter, happier, and more energetic making you last longer throughout the day.

583. There is a small village in India called "Shani Shingapur" which has three hundred buildings that have no doors to them. People leave their businesses, homes and schools open as they believe anyone who does steal anything will face seven years of bad luck.

584. A rainbow grilled cheese sandwich is one of the specials at the

Chomp Eatery Restaurant in Los Angeles. In the sandwich, the blue tastes like lavender, the green like basil, the red like tomatoes, and the yellow tastes like plain cheese.

585. Russia has created a capsule that treats alcoholism. It's implanted under the skin and causes chemicals to release. This leads the user to feel nauseous, out of breath, and mental confusion when alcohol is consumed.

586. In China, in order to draw tourists to the panda base in Chengdu, a large panda bear conservation facility, a panda themed subway train was created.

587. In the film "Pulp Fiction," the scene where John Travolta gives the adrenaline shot to Uma Thurman's chest was shot in reverse with the actor pulling the needle away. A fake chest was bought from a special effects company by director Quentin Tarantino, but he later decided just to use that trick instead.

588. It's against the honor code to consume alcohol for Brigham Young University students. For that reason the university holds a Milktober Fest, as an alternative to Oktoberfest, where they promote drinking milk and doing homework before the midterm season.

589. There are very few non-extinct mammals that are venomous, and male platypuses are among them. Evidently, their venom causes excruciating pain that is resistant to painkillers and has long lasting effects, but it's non-lethal to humans. They secrete the venom from hind leg spurs during their breeding season.

590. In Japan, there is a town called "Nagoro" that has more scarecrows than people. The town has around thirty people and over 400 scarecrows.

591. Jens Stoltenberg, a former Norwegian Prime Minister, once drove a taxi around because he wanted to hear what real Norwegian voters had to say. He thought that taxis were actually one of the few places where people can freely share their opinions.

592. Julio Cortazar published a book named "Hopscotch" in 1966, which is over a hundred and fifty chapters long and makes sense no matter which chapter you begin reading from.

593. "Frito feet" is the term coined for when a pet dog's paws smell

oddly of corn chips. The yeasty odor is actually caused by bacteria the canine has picked up.

594. Blood type in dogs is different from the types found in humans. Although there are six main blood types, 42% of dogs have the same type, which is universal.

595. In the film adaptation of the video game Super Mario Bros, actor Tom Hanks auditioned for the role of Mario.

596. In Williamstown, Kentucky, there's a replica of Noah's Ark that was built by the Creationist Ministry. Its dimensions are exactly as indicated in the book of Genesis at 450 feet (137 meters) long, sixty seven feet (twenty meters) high, and forty six feet (fourteen meters) wide. It cost approximately $100 million to make.

597. There is a protein found in the vampire bat's saliva that acts as an anticoagulant; it helps to keep their victim's blood flowing while they feed. Researchers have actually been studying the protein to see if it can help dissolve blood clots and help with stroke victims.

598. Rajendra Singh from India is known as the water man of the country. He managed to revive five rivers and brought water back to 1,000 villages in India using native water preservation techniques.

599. Putting aside the Earth's 18.6 miles (thirty kilometers) per second revolution around the sun, all things located along the equator are moving at about 990 miles (1,600 kilometers) per hour, while all things located at the north and south poles are basically stationary, only spinning in its position.

600. Sea cucumbers can mutilate their own bodies when feeling threatened, as a defense mechanism. They are able to violently contract their muscles and jettison some of their internal organs out of their anus. The missing body parts are later rapidly regenerated.

601. Palacio de Sal Resort is a hotel in Bolivia made up of one million fourteen inch (thirty five centimeter) blocks of compressed grains of salt. The furniture is also made out of salt.

602. Boiling water in a paper cup is actually possible, by holding it over a stove at a proper distance from the flame.

603. All human embryos start off as females in the womb, and the reason why men have nipples.

604. When bobsledding was developed in the 1880's, the earliest participants in the sport would bob their heads trying to gain speed, and that's how it got its name. As it turned, bobbing one's head didn't really help people gain speed, but the name stuck anyway.

605. Rosa Abbott was the only female passenger that went down with the Titanic who survived. She was a third class passenger.

606. The very last McDonald's hamburger and fries sold in Iceland is on display at a bus hostel in Reykjavik. You can watch real-time footage of it over a live stream. It has been there since October 30 of 2009 when a man bought it and left it there.

607. Three months after Charlie Chaplin died, his corpse was stolen by two auto mechanics who intended to extort money from his family. The thieves were later caught and Chaplin's body was found eleven weeks later. To avoid similar attempts later on, his body was reburied under concrete.

608. Ester Okade is a ten year old girl who is already enrolled in university. She had the highest exam scores in her class and had mastered algebra when she was only four years old.

609. "Something Store" is an online shop that for $10 will randomly select an item and send it to you, and only know what you get once you receive the item.

610. Two radio stations in San Francisco had to ban Lorde's hit song "Royals" during the World Series in 2014, when the Kansas City Royals were pitted against the San Francisco Giants, because angry Giants fans called in and emailed the stations to complain about the song.

611. The powerful drum reverb entrance in the song "In the Air Tonight" by Phil Collins was actually an accident. While Collins was playing drums for another song for Peter Gabriel's third solo album, the reverse talk back was unintentionally activated and left on.

612. The piercing screeching sound that many, particularly in

America, associate with the bald eagle, isn't from the eagle at all. Hollywood wanted to make the eagle, the symbol of America, sound more fierce, so they frequently dub the screech of the red-tailed hawk onto the bald eagle. The actual bald eagle doesn't sound like a tough predator swooping in from the sky, but more like a singing parakeet.

613. Bradley Corporation, an international manufacturer of commercial hand washing products, conducted a Healthy Hand Washing Survey that revealed that only 66% of Americans wash their hands after using a public washroom, while almost 70% of them admitted to skip the soap.

614. "Somebody to love" was Freddy Mercury's favorite song, however, he didn't tell anyone that because he didn't want everyone to know he liked his own music.

615. The largest species of earthworm in the world can measure up to ten feet (three meters) long. It can be found in Gippsland, in southeastern Australia.

616. When it comes to long-distance running, humans are the best on the planet. We can outrun every animal on the planet and run in conditions that no other animal can run in.

617. Throughout the filming of "The Hobbit" trilogy, twenty seven animals died on set. Some of them fell into sink holes while other smaller ones, like chickens, were killed by unsupervised dogs. As a result, PETA made a global protest on the trilogy.

618. There is a dog named Body that makes almost two hundred thousand dollars a year by modeling clothes on Instagram.

619. In 1967, the world's first UFO landing pad was built in St. Paul, Alberta, Canada. The 130-ton structure has a raised platform with a map of Canada imprinted on the backstop consisting of stones provided by each province in Canada. The pad also has a time capsule that is scheduled to be opened on the one hundred year anniversary of the pad's opening, which is in 2067.

620. Every December since 1960, between finals and the end of the semester, volunteers at a dorm at the University of Illinois will sing you a Christmas carol upon request. All you have to do is call Dial-A-Carol at (217) 332-1882, any time and any day after

finals and before the end of the semester, and they will sing you a carol.

621. In 1927, Pez was invented in Vienna, Austria, as a breath mint. The name is actually an abbreviation for the German word "pfefferminz," which means peppermint.

622. There was a safety net put up under the Golden Gate Bridge while it was being constructed. It saved nineteen men and they became known as the "Halfway to Hell Club."

623. Actress Margaret Hamilton, who is mostly remembered for playing the scary wicked witch in The Wizard of Oz and terrifying children everywhere, was actually a kindergarten teacher before she started her acting career.

624. In 2012, a chain of 228 people paid for the customer behind them at a Tim Hortons in Winnipeg. The act of kindness and generosity lasted for about three hours, after someone broke the chain by paying only for their coffee and not the customers behind them.

625. About 30% of all the food that Americans eat is actually pollinated by honeybees as well as 85% of all flowering plants. Honeybees are also responsible for 90% of the pollen that is transferred to and from our orchard crops. Unfortunately, 70% of the feral honeybee population has disappeared or died.

626. Doctor Fareed Farah, an oncologist from Michigan, was sentenced to forty five years in prison after finding out that he had milked 553 cancer patients for millions of dollars. He was accused of overtreating, undertreating, misdiagnosing, and even administering treatment to people that never had cancer in the first place.

627. Around 300 B.C., turkeys were a symbol of power to the ancient Mayans, so they used to worship them like gods. They believed that they had supernatural abilities; as a result, they were exclusively owned by the most rich and powerful people.

628. "Vinculum" is the name given to the line that separates the top and bottom numbers of a fraction.

629. The youngest person to ever climb Mount Everest was Jordan Romero, in 2010, at the age of thirteen. While at the summit, he called his mom from a satellite phone and left a rabbit's foot

there. He also planted seeds a Buddhist monk gave him at a monastery.

630. Most fruits grow on trees. Pineapples, however, grow on shrubs; and each pineapple plant only grows one pineapple.

631. Treating a heroin addiction in The United States has a five year cost of \$318,500, while an Oxycodone addiction is \$132,405.

632. Sudarsan Pattnaik created the tallest sandcastle in the world on February 10, 2017, on Puri Beach in Odisha, India. The sandcastle took nine days to complete, it was forty eight feet (fourteen meters) high and it had a 529 feet (161 meter) wide circular base.

633. At the Marine Mammal Studies Institute in Mississippi, dolphins were trained to bring trash back that fell into the pools in exchange for fish. Kelly, one of the smartest dolphins, hid pieces of paper under a rock and tore off smaller paper pieces in order to get more fish out of it.

634. Patients with Parkinson's were given placebos and those who believed it was medicine worth \$1,500, showed more positive results than patients who were told they were getting a drug worth \$100, according to a study published in the Journal of Neurology. In both cases, the doctors only gave them saline shots.

635. Dog saliva was considered to be medicinal by the ancient Mesopotamians. They documented that when a dog licked their wounds, the recovery process was faster.

636. In order to ward off evil spirits, ancient Egyptians would rim their eyes with kohl, a mixture of lead, copper, burned almonds, and soot.

637. All citizens' tax returns in Norway are publicly available as they are posted online, showing their total income and total taxes paid. So if you want to gossip on your neighbor or any other person's income, you can do it; the only thing is that they will receive an email letting them know that you were snooping.

638. The world's slowest mammal is the sloth. Due to its sedentary character, algae grow on its coat giving it a greenish tinge that helps camouflage them in trees.

639. During World War II, the Nazis attempted to teach dogs how to talk and read, and even had special academies for trainees, according to Dr. Jan Bondeson, from Cardiff University. It was reported that one dog said the words "mind furor" when asked who Adolf Hitler was.

640. One hookah session delivers about twenty five times the tar, two and a half times the nicotine, and ten times the carbon monoxide if compared to one cigarette.

641. In order to pass the height requirements of 5'8" (1.76 meters), sumo wrestlers in Japan used to get silicone implants on top of their heads.

642. The largest eyes ever studied in the animal kingdom belong to the colossal squid, measuring almost eleven inches (twenty seven centimeters), almost the same size as a volleyball. In fact, researchers believe that they may be the largest eyes that ever existed.

643. The United States Playing Card Company in collaboration with the American and British intelligence agencies created a very special deck of cards during World War II with the intention of helping prisoners of war escape from German POW camps. The deck was called the "map" deck and it was made by hiding maps of top secret escape routes between the two paper layers that make up regular playing cards. When the cards were soaked in water, they could be peeled apart to reveal hidden maps that allowed escaping prisoners to find their way to safety.

644. The longest word that is typed with only the left hand on the keyboard is stewardesses.

645. It takes fifty hours of socializing to go from an acquaintance to a casual friend, according to a recent study by the University of Kansas. To become a real friend, it takes another forty hours, and a total of 200 hours to become a close friend.

646. The only river in the world that crosses the Equator twice is the Congo River by flowing north and south of it. It's also the only major river in the world that crosses the Equator even once.

647. In Japan, October 10 is considered Tom Cruise Day, as per a 2006 declaration. The Japan Memorial Day Association said

that the actor received that honor because he visited the country more often than any other Hollywood star.

648. Legendary author Ernest Hemingway survived lots of unfortunate things in his life, including two plane crashes. He also suffered from skin cancer, malaria, anthrax, dysentery, hepatitis, pneumonia, a ruptured liver, a ruptured kidney, a ruptured spleen, a cracked skull, and a broken vertebra.

649. The last verse of the hit song "Sitting on the Dock of the Bay" was whistled by singer Otis Redding because he didn't have the words written for it when it was recorded. His plan was to fill in the verse, but he unfortunately died in a plane crash three days after recording it. The producer, however, decided to leave the whistling in.

650. On December 12, 1925, the first motel ever opened in San Luis Obispo, California, and was called the "Milestone Inn." The purpose of the motel was to lodge automobile travelers, which is the main reason they are called motels.

651. During the filming of Rocky IV, Sylvester Stallone spent nine days in intensive care at hospital because of Dolph Lundgren. During a fight scene, Dolph hit him so hard in the chest that the pericardial sac around his heart swelled up, which impeded the beating of his heart and caused his blood pressure to skyrocket to 290.

652. In January 2016, a new species of hermit crab was accidentally discovered by underwater photographer Ellen Mueller at the National Marine Park of the southern Caribbean island of Bonaire. It has been called the "Candy Striped Hermit Crab" because its legs look like candy canes.

653. To establish which pets cared more about their owners, Dr. Paul Zack did a neuroscience experiment in 2016 where he checked the levels of oxytocin, the love hormone, in cats and dogs after they played with their owners. He found that the hormone increased by just 12% in cats, but in dogs, it increased by an average of 57%.

654. In order to hide from predators and also sneak up on prey, the praying mantis can actually camouflage itself by changing

color. It can vary from dark brown to green to blend in with tree bark and leaves.

655. American President Calvin Coolidge had a pet raccoon named Rebecca. She was originally supposed to be eaten at their 1926 White House Thanksgiving dinner, however, the family found her to be friendly and docile, so they decided to keep her as a pet instead.

656. Dan and Caren Mahar, a New York couple, had their child diagnosed with xeroderma pigmentosum, a condition in which exposure to sunlight causes third-degree burns and cancer. The couple soon founded Camp Sundown, a summer camp for kids suffering the genetic disorder where all camp activities are held after sundown.

657. There are thousands of microscopic mites living on your face right now. There are actually two species: demodex folliculorum that live in your pores and hair follicles; and D. brevis that settle deeper in the oily sebaceous glands in your face.

658. French philosopher Voltaire was asked to renounce Satan on his deathbed in 1778. He replied: "Now isn't the time to be making new enemies."

659. The only airport in the world where a schedule of flights take off and land on a beach is Barra Airport, in Scotland.

660. Due to the lack of gravity in space, astronauts tears coagulate in the eyes and end up stinging. In 2011, astronaut Andrew Feustel got some anti-fogging solution stuck in his eye and tears weren't going to get it out, so he had to rub his eyes on the foam inside of this helmet.

661. "The Lion King" was originally called "The King of the Jungle." The Disney team later learned that lions don't live in jungles, so they renamed it.

662. Barbara Soaper, from Michigan, gave birth to her three children on 08/08/08, 09/09/09, and 10/10/10 respectively. The odds of this happening are fifty million to one.

663. During his college days at William and Mary, comedian Jon Stewart was a walk-on soccer player. He even scored the only

goal in the game that drove the team to the NCAA tournament.

664. The fear of long words is called "hippopotomonstrosesquippedaliophobia."

665. Back in 1962, Tom Monaghan, the founder of Domino's Pizza, met his wife on his very first pizza delivery.

666. In Australia, there is a cave called "Well It Wasn't There Last Year Cave."

667. If the parents of a baby squirrel die, other squirrels will adopt the baby.

668. Air India Flight 216 took off from Evansville, Indiana, and crashed almost immediately, killing the entire University of Evansville basketball team with the exception of one member, on December 13, 1977. The surviving team member wasn't even on the flight. Two weeks after the plane crush, he died after he was hit by a drunk driver.

669. There are some animals that are immune to the venom of the black widow spider, such as sheep and rabbits.

670. The largest living crocodile in captivity, the Australian saltwater, is eighteen feet (5.5 meters) long according to the Guinness World Records. It's also considered as the most fearsome of today's species; they can live for more than 100 years, grow up to twenty-three feet (seven meters), and weigh more than one ton.

671. Bill Wilson, the co-founder of Alcoholics Anonymous, thought that using LSD could help treat alcoholism based on his own experiences with the drug. In fact, he suggested incorporating the drug into the program, but the other leading members refused.

672. Grace Brett is a 104 year old knitter who yarn-bombed her town. She is thought to be the world's oldest street artist.

673. The majority of car airbags can deploy at speeds of up to 200 miles (322 kilometers) per hour. At speeds that high, airbags can cause real harm to a car occupant, and it can break one's bones.

674. Research shows that people's voices change when they find

someone attractive. The changes in vocal tones are subtle and the speaker isn't aware of the unconscious change.

675. For Yao Ming's debut game in the NBA, his team promoted the game by giving out over eight thousand fortune cookies. Yao Ming wasn't offended at all since he'd never seen one before in China, and thought it was an American invention.

676. In California, the breeding of killer whales in captivity is now illegal. They have also banned killer whales to perform in shows just for entertainment.

677. Guinea pigs are very lonely and social creatures. Hence, in New Zealand, it's illegal to own just one. In fact, they have matchmaking companies that match up your guinea pig if their partner dies, which is part of a sweeping animals' rights legislation that was first introduced in 2008.

678. President Theodore Roosevelt didn't like the idea of putting "In God We Trust" on US currency. He thought it would be unwise to cheapen such a motto by using it on coins, the same as using it on postage stamps or in advertisements.

679. Based on a study done by researchers from Macquarie University, people with psychopathic inclinations have a poor sense of smell.

680. Fazal Din, a twenty three year old Indian soldier was in Burma, commanding an attack on Japan's bunker position when, on March 2, 1945, at the height of the Second World War, he found himself stabbed all the way through by a Japanese sword. As the enemy soldier pulled it out to move on, Din grabbed the sword from his hand, then used it to kill him and another soldier. He waved the sword in the air to inspire his platoon, then he walked twenty five yards to the platoon headquarters, bleeding along the way, where he calmly gave his report upon arrival, before he collapsed and died a hero.

681. George Washington was promoted to history's only six star general in 1976.

682. It's harder to get into the new Apple store in New York than it is to get into Harvard. Only 7% of applicants get accepted into Harvard while Apple's acceptance rate is only 2%.

683. In 1999, a man named Cornelius Anderson helped in robbing a Burger King and was sentenced to serve thirteen years in prison, but no one ever came to collect him so he continued on living his life. Twelve years later the police were preparing for his release only to realize that they never arrested him to begin with.

684. Fifteen days before or after a solar eclipse, there is always a lunar eclipse.

685. If you cry in outer space, your tears never fall; they just stay under your eye, like a blob.

686. In order to accommodate racial segregation laws, the Pentagon was built with extra bathrooms.

687. Similarly to our earthquakes, there are moonquakes on the moon, with the difference that they are weaker and less common. In fact, there are four known types: deep moonquakes, shallow moonquakes, thermal moonquakes, and meteorite moonquakes.

688. A group of hippos is called a crash. A group of emus is called a mob. A group of crows is called a murder. A group of zebras is called a zeal. A group of apes is called a shrewdness. A group of giraffes is called a tower. And a group of bears is called a sleuth.

689. Honey bees have five eyes: two compound eyes that help them see around themselves at the same time, and three simple eyes situated on the top of their heads that help them with orientation.

690. Between 1860 and 1916, it was mandatory that every soldier in the British Army had a mustache. If someone shaved it, he would be disciplined or even imprisoned. In battle, facial hair has its advantages as it protects the soldier's face from the cold elements.

691. In London, there is a music ticketing app called "Dice" that allows their employees to call out of work for being too hangover. They simply send a message to their boss with beer, music, and sick emoji. Each employee is permitted to take four hangover days a year.

692. The independent Disney princess Merida from the animated

movie Brave is the only Disney princess who neither sang nor had a love interest in her movie.

693. The alligators in Southern Florida greatly outnumber crocodiles. It's the only place on the planet where you can find gators and crocs coexisting in the wild.

694. The "Taxi Fabric Project" in Mumbai, India, has upcoming designers reupholster and transform taxi cab interiors.

695. In June 2011, the first pinball-inspired skate park was built by Mountain Dew in Henderson, New Zealand. It's named the Mountain Dew Skate Pinball Park which features an interactive skate park with sensors triggering lights, sounds, and skill level scoring on the top board.

696. When singers Taylor Swift, Miley Cyrus, and Katy Perry met in a dressing room at the Grammy Awards, Katy asked the other two for locks of their hair. They both obliged, and Katy wrapped both clippings in a ribbon, and put them in her handbag.

697. The "PT" in PT Cruiser stands for "personal transport."

698. In 1987, a lifetime unlimited first-class American Airlines ticket costing $250,000 was bought by Steve Rothstein. He flew over 10,000 flights with the same ticket, costing the company some $21 million. The company terminated his ticket in 2008.

699. Every year, over two million job applications are received by Google from around the world. As of February 2019, they had more than 114,000 employees.

700. Since 2017, San Francisco is the first city in the United States to offer free college.

701. Takuya Nagaya, a twenty three year old man from Japan, started to slither on the floor saying that he had become a snake. His parents thought that he had been possessed by a snake, so his father Katsumi spent the next two days head butting and biting his son to "drive out the snake," causing his death in the process.

702. Soviet geologists discovered a family in the middle of Serbia in 1978 that hadn't seen another human in over forty two years.

703. The weight of all the electrons in motion that make up the Internet at any given time is equal to fifty grams according to

BSOS. In other words, the Internet is estimated to weigh about the same as a medium sized egg or a strawberry.

704. There is a lake in Victoria, Australia, that can glow in the dark. The light is created when microorganisms in the water are disturbed which creates a chemical reaction called bioluminescence.

705. Lake Baikal in Siberia is the deepest lake in the world at over 5,382 feet (1,641 meters) deep. It's also the most voluminous freshwater lake on Earth, containing nearly 20% of the world's unfrozen fresh water.

706. Xiong Shulhua, a millionaire Chinese businessman, demolished entire rundown huts in his native village and decided to build luxury flats. Later he gave the keys to the residents for free.

707. After cardiovascular disease, cancer is the second leading cause of death in the world. Every sixth death in the world is caused by cancer.

708. According to records, Australian jewel beetles have been observed to attempt to mate with empty beer bottles instead of females because of the bottle's brown color. This has led to a reduced survival rate for them.

709. The informal pronunciation of probably is "proly," which originated in the 1940's.

710. When dogs are pooping, they feel more vulnerable so they look at their owners for protection.

711. Since 1967, Tiffany has manufactured the Vince Lombardi trophy, which is awarded annually to the winners of the Super Bowl. The 20.7 inches (52.7 centimeter) tall trophy is a football standing upright on a three-sided stand, and is made completely of sterling silver. It weighs just over 6.6 pounds (three kilograms) and is worth over $25,000.

712. Based on the mood that it's experiencing, the sailfish changes the color of its skin. When they hunt for prey, they become darker. When they are excited or tired, they become neon and copper colored.

713. Gypsum or white mineral spar used to be extracted from the bed of Niagara River and some traders sold it to tourists who

were led to believe that they were bits of petrified mist that came from the Niagara Falls.

714. The sports television channel ESPN is actually owned by Disney with a majority ownership of 80%. Disney also owns Pixar, ABC Broadcasting Company, Lucasfilm, Marvel, A&E, and the History Channel.

715. In 1912, HersheyPark in Hershey, Philadelphia, installed a new merry-go-round, and the guy hired to paint the amusement park signs wrote "CARROUSEL" instead of spelling it correctly without the additional "R." Rather than repainting the signs, the park chose to operate the ride using that name for the next thirty two years.

716. Samsung, the huge manufacturer of TVs, cell phones, and home appliances, began as a grocery store.

717. In the books written by Sir Arthur Conan Doyle, Sherlock Holmes never says the phrase "elementary, my dear Watson." Basil Rathorn actually said the line in the 1939 film "The Adventures of Sherlock Holmes."

718. Peter Robbins, the original voice actor of Charlie Brown, is currently in prison for threatening the manager of a mobile home park that he lived in.

719. Greyfriars Bobby is a dog that sat by his owner's grave in Scotland for fourteen years until he eventually died.

720. The average American consumes between 149 and 169 pounds (sixty eight and seventy seven kilograms) of refined sugar every year, according to the Department of Agriculture. This means that for every American who eats 4.4 pounds (two kilograms) of sugar a year, there is one who eats 293 pounds (133 kilograms) a year.

721. Actor Charlie Sheen once spent over six thousand dollars to buy twenty five hundred seats at a baseball game in attempts to catch a home-run ball.

722. Crescent Lake is an oasis located in the middle of the Gobi Desert, 3.7 miles (5.9 kilometers) from the outskirts of the city of Dunhuang, in western China. It is believed to have been there for over 2,000 years.

723. The most expensive liquid on Earth is scorpion venom valued

at almost forty million dollars per gallon. You'd have to milk two and a half million scorpions to obtain a whole gallon of liquid.

724. As Mel Brooks, the legendary filmmaker and comedian, placed his handprints in his Hollywood Walk of Fame star, he added an eleventh prosthetic finger to one hand.

725. On March 12, 1912, Juliette Gordon Low founded the Girl Scouts in Savannah, Georgia. Today, there are about 2.7 million Girl Scouts, 1.9 million girl members, and 800,000 adult members.

726. Back in 1920, Hans Riegel created the gummy bear candies, initially called dancing bears. They were originally made out of licorice.

727. NASA astronaut Scott Kelly spent almost a year living aboard the International Space Station. When he came back home, he found out he was two inches (five centimeters) taller than his identical twin brother Mark. Due to gravity, the disks of the spinal column get compressed on Earth. So in space, as there is no gravity, the disks actually expand and the spine lengthens, making astronauts taller.

728. In the 1908 Olympics, American sprinter Forrest Smithson ran the 110-meter hurdles while carrying a Bible in his hand, winning the gold medal. He apparently did this as a way to protest against the decision to run the finals on Sundays. The truth however was that he was so religious that he often ran with a Bible.

729. In San Francisco, there is a fire hydrant that survived the 1906 earthquake, helping firefighters to save the mission district. In memory of the event, it was painted gold.

730. Zoe is a very unique white zebra that has light golden stripes and blue eyes due to a condition known as amelanosis. She lives at Hawaii's Three Ring Ranch animal sanctuary.

731. The magician Teller from Penn and Teller began performing in silence. In his youth, he used to do shows at college fraternity parties and found out that if he stayed quiet throughout the act, he was least likely to get beer poured on him or heckled. Penn Jillette never knew how to play poker until eight days

before his appearance on the show Celebrity Poker Showdown in 2004.

732. Heteropaternal superfecundation is a very rare phenomenon that occurs when two twins have two different fathers. Only a few cases have been documented worldwide.

733. When Twitter first came out, Adele was known for tweeting while drunk. She is not allowed to send out her own tweets anymore.

734. When rabbits are born, they are furless, blind, and too weak to move by themselves. Hares on the other hand are born with lots of hair, can immediately see, and are strong enough to start bouncing around right after birth.

735. The Bios Incube is an invention created by Bios Urn. It's a type of incubator that monitors and cultivates trees from human ashes in people's homes. So instead of keeping your departed loved one in an urn on the fireplace mantle, now you can keep them in the form of a tree.

736. A scooter slash stroller hybrid was developed by Austrian inventor Valentin Vodev. By just clicking a button, the stroller transforms into a scooter and can travel as fast as ten miles (sixteen kilometers) per hour.

737. Katy Hudson was the name of singer Katy Perry's debut album. She originally went by this name and although the album was overall well-reviewed by critics, only 200 copies were sold. The record label she recorded it on eventually had to close, and Katy Hudson became who we all know as Katy Perry today.

738. In the UK, a robotic rectum has been created by researchers for proctologists to practice their physical rectal exams. It allows medical professions to learn without the use of real life volunteers.

739. During the 1961 to 1962 NBA season, Wilt Chamberlain averaged a mind-boggling 50.4 points per game for the Philadelphia Warriors. He also scored 100 points in a game during the same season on March 2, 1962.

740. The famous sound made by cicadas is actually only produced by males. Their organs have something called tymbals; their

muscles pop the tymbals in and out creating that well-known sound.

741. From 1986 to 1988, Clint Eastwood was the Mayor of Carmel, California. His salary was $200 a month.

742. A man who was morbidly obese took part in an experimental fast in 1965. He was only given potassium tablets and multivitamins. He lost 273.4 pounds (124 kilograms) as a result.

743. The producers of the Disney film "The Lion King" asked the musical group Abba to write the songs, but they turned it down as they were not available. They ended up asking their second favorite choice, Elton John.

744. One of the most deadly venoms in the world is found in the box jellyfish. Human victims can sometimes drown of heart failure from the pain and shock, and survivors can feel significant pain for weeks after. They also often leave scarring on the body area where the tentacle made contact.

745. In 2005, comedian Tim FitzHigham rode across the English Channel in a copper bathtub for charity, setting a world record as the first bathtub crosser of the English Channel.

746. The phrase "hakuna matata" was trademarked by Walt Disney Company for clothing, headgear, and footwear.

747. Studies conducted at Turkey's Ataturk University and the University of Manchester have shown that dogs and cats are right or left pawed, just like humans are right or left handed.

748. According to scientist Martin Banks from the University of California, Berkeley, animals with vertical slits as pupils are likely to be an ambush predator. As these animals need to correctly judge the distance between them and their prey, having vertical slits actually optimizes that ability.

749. Owls are actually unable to roll or move their eyes and instead turn their heads in order to look sideways. Some owls are even able to turn their heads up to 270 degrees.

750. In Australia, Weird Al Yankovic's song "Eat It" reached number one on the music charts, while Michael Jackson's song "Beat It" surprisingly only went as high as number three.

751. Joe Dougherty provided the original voice of Porky Pig; he also had a stutter familiar to the character on screen. However, he

was unable to get his own stuttering under control and missed cues, hence causing delays. In 1937, he was replaced by legendary voice actor Mel Blanc, who took over the role for fifty two years.

752. In order to avoid euthanization, about fifty cats and dogs are transported from Houston to Colorado every week.

753. Based on the State Health Department records, Hawaii's visitor drowning rate is thirteen times higher than the national average over the past decade, and ten times the rate of the number of its own inhabitants.

754. In January 2017, a craft beer maker known as the Veil Brewing Company in Richmond, Virginia, created a new beer that was infused with Oreo cookies. They took their chocolate milk stout and conditioned it with hundreds of Oreo cookies, naming it "Horn Swaddler Chocolate Milk Stout with Oreos."

755. Cyber-homeless refers to a class of people in Japan who live at cyber cafes, as they are a cheaper alternative for housing. The cyber cafes offer free showers to customers and also sell underwear.

756. The oldest continuously used national flag according to the Guinness World Records is the Dannebrog or Danish cloth, the flag for Denmark, which has been in use since the 1370's.

757. The song Sussudio by Phil Collins was based on a made up word. When he couldn't think of actual lyrics to fill the line, he just left it in as the chorus and title.

758. Kanye West invited Seth Rogen to give him feedback on all his tracks on his new album when Rogen released a parody on the "Bound 2" music video.

759. The first official coin to go into circulation in the US was created by Benjamin Franklin. Instead of it saying "In God We Trust" it said "Mind Your Business."

760. In August of 2016, a Tasmanian woman gave birth to her first baby at sixty three years old, making her Australia's oldest new mother.

761. A picture of a nine year old boy named Daniel Cabrera, from the Philippines doing his homework in the street, assisted by the light of a local McDonald's became so viral that

donations around the world were sent including money, school supplies, and a college scholarship to both him and his family.

762. Infamous drug lord Pablo Escobar had his own private zoo with about 200 animals. He used his drug planes to smuggle many of the animals into the country.

763. Jets in the sky leave a white trail across it for the same reason that you can see your breath in the winter. It's carbon dioxide and water creating visible moisture.

764. In ancient Rome, Belladonna plants were used as ingredients in drops to make women's eyes larger. These plants are also known as "Deadly Nightshade" due to being quite lethal even in small quantities. Nowadays, it is still used by doctors to dilate patients' eyes.

765. In Bangalore, India, there is a lake called Bellandur Lake. It is so toxic that it's covered in froth and sometimes bursts into flames. The foam on it is the result of toxic water which has a high amount of ammonia and phosphate, and very low dissolved oxygen, as the result of many years of untreated chemical waste going into it. Given the amount of grease, oil, and detergent in the froth, it often catches fire.

766. A biotech startup has succeeded in printing 3D rhino horns that are genetically similar to a real horn. The company plans to flood Chinese and Vietnamese markets, where demand is often high, and bring down the price, and hopefully the demand.

767. In the Mojave Desert, California, there is a solar power plant that covers 1.56 square miles (2.5 square kilometers). It's actually the largest solar power plant in the world.

768. In 2009, the Free Little Library, a nonprofit organization, began to operate by offering free books in many little libraries in communities all over the world. Today there are over 50,000 book exchanges worldwide.

769. The highest life expectancy in the world is found in Japan, at almost eighty four years on average. Okinawa Island has much to do with it as it's known for having some of the longest-living people in the entire world. The island houses thirty four

centenarians per 100,000 people, which is more than three times the rate of mainland Japan.

770. The Galapagos Islands are a chain of islands created by volcanic activity. The islands house a great variety of fauna species, although no animals are actually native to the Galapagos. Every species of animal there came from floating on ocean or air currents.

771. Chicken eggs as well as other bird eggs have tiny holes or pores on them, which allow baby birds to breathe in oxygen and get rid of carbon dioxide. A chicken egg, for example, has more than 7,000 pores.

772. The metallic smell you get from smelling money coins is the result of your body's oils breaking down in the presence of iron or copper. If you use a paper towel to pick up a penny, however, you can tell there is no odor.

773. Jim Henson, the Muppets creator, believed in allowing a character to grow organically. His viewpoint was that each Muppet had a distinct personality. He even thought that it was the job of the puppeteer to uncover it.

774. In July of 2018, a horn shark was stolen by three thieves from an aquarium in San Antonio. They masked it as a baby before putting it in a stroller and wheeling it out. Eventually, two of the thieves confessed to the police and were sentenced.

775. Dogs love the herb anise the same way that cats love catnip. In fact, anise is the scent used on the artificial rabbit in greyhound races to get the dogs to run.

776. The name LEGO comes from the abbreviation of the two Danish words "leg godt" which mean "play well."

777. Antonio Lopez De Santa Anna, who was a Mexican general in 1838, was hit by cannon fire, so his leg had to be amputated. Four years after this happened, the general did a weird thing; he asked for his leg to be exhumed so it could be buried again with full military honors in a funeral service that included prayers and speeches. It was finally buried under a spectacular monument in Santa Paula Cemetery, inside a crystal vase.

778. From the 1980's until the 1990's, the Italian mafia trafficked nuclear waste and ended up dumping it in Somalia.

82

779. Around five million dollars an episode and more than 100 million dollars overall were turned down by Jerry Seinfeld just to run a tenth season of Seinfeld. The amount was three times more than anyone on television had ever been offered at the time.

780. The population density in Siberia is less than eight people per one square mile (2.5 square kilometers). Although Siberia covers 77% of all of Russia and has an area of more than fifty times that of the UK, it is barely populated.

781. Wolves work together and communicate with each other to make decisions as a group. Dogs however operate under a strict hierarchy.

782. In 2016, a teacup and saucer used by Lady Gaga sold at an auction for almost $74,000. The cup was marked with her lipstick bearing the Japanese message: "We pray for Japan" along with her autograph. The money went to charity.

783. Dr. Bhakti Yadav is a ninety one year old Indian gynecologist who has been treating patients for decades. She started her career in 1948, just a year after India's independence.

784. The Tower of Hercules, in Spain, is the oldest lighthouse in the world. It was erected in the first century and is still operational.

785. The King of Yugoslavia, Alexander the first, refused to go to any events on a Tuesday since three of his family members had died on this day of the week. When he was finally convinced that nothing would happen, he made an appearance on a Tuesday in October of 1934, and was assassinated.

786. President Abraham Lincoln suffered from heavy depression. He refused to carry a knife, as most men used to do, because he was afraid that he would harm himself. In the summer of 1835 and in the winter of 1840, he went through major depressing episodes.

787. Elvis Presley failed music class in high school.

788. After many tests, a team of researchers at Michigan State University have created a transparent solar panel that can be used in buildings to potentially power the entire building. It can also be retrofitted to older glass buildings to harness power.

789. In New York City's Central Park, there are about 18,000 different kinds of trees.

790. Scientists found out in March, 2018, that all galaxies rotate at the rate of a billion years for a single spin, and it's the same irrespective of the size of the individual galaxy.

791. In the 1960's, the Fly Geyser was accidentally created by a power company in Nevada's Black Rock Desert. They did this by drilling into a geothermic pocket that let loose a stream of oil, water, and calcium deposits. Today, it's a vibrant, living sculpture that is always changing due to the colorful algae in the water.

792. The only member of the canine family that hibernates is the raccoon dog, so it needs to load up on food before winter arrives.

793. The word "BASE" as in "base jumping" is an acronym for four categories of fixed objects from which you can jump. They are building, antenna, span, and Earth.

794. Patients in hospitals who have a view of trees and natural scenery recover faster than those who do not, according to the American Association for the Advancement of Science. Experts gathered this information between the years of 1972 and 1981, by observing patients who stayed in a particular suburban Pennsylvania hospital.

795. Rats are very flexible. An adult rat can fit through a hole as small as a quarter, or a gap less than one inch (2.5 centimeters) wide. This is how they can easily invade your home without your knowledge.

796. As of 2018, the United States Department of Defense employs 2.86 million people from military, National Guard, and civilian backgrounds. The annual budget for the Department of Defense is $7.17 billion US.

797. The wels catfish is the largest freshwater fish in Europe according to National Geographic explorer Zeb Hogan. It can grow up to fifteen feet (4.5 meters) long, weigh as much as 660 pounds (299 kilograms), and live for decades, even as long as eighty years.

798. Tigers' tongues are very coarse and can actually lick flesh down to the bone.
799. "Sock City" is another name given to the town of Detang in China, as they produce eight billion pairs of socks every year. This represents one third of the socks made worldwide.
800. In order to avoid being hit by lethal-sized space debris, the International Space Station had to be moved three separate times in 2014.
801. There are countries with literacy rates of almost 100%, such as Andorra, Finland, Greenland, Lichtenstein, Luxembourg, and Norway. In general, governments of these countries require by law that every young child shows a compulsory attendance within its school systems. Moreover, some provide free schooling up to the secondary level of education and, along with a higher percentage of its GDP being allotted for the education sector, has resulted in higher literacy rates.
802. In 1950, Himalayan and American black bears were used as test subjects by the United States Air Force when testing their ejector seats for the B-58 Hustle. The bears were sedated and strapped into the seats. Despite some of them suffering broken bones, all of them survived until they were euthanized and dissected.
803. In June of 2015, the pacu fish was found in New Jersey. It's a type of fish native to South America, that's a flesh-eating kind of piranha known for its unique teeth, which bear a peculiar similarity to human teeth. Luckily, it's considered mostly harmless to humans as it primarily eats plants.
804. In Port Vila, Vanuatu, at the Hideaway Island Resort and Marine Sanctuary there is an underwater post office, the only one of its kind in the world. Snorkelers and divers can post special waterproof postcards in ten feet (three meters) of water.
805. The world's biggest meat eaters are Australians, followed by Americans. On average, Australians consume 200 pounds (ninety one kilograms) per year, while Americans consume just a bit under that at 198 pounds (eighty nine kilograms) a year.
806. In 2008, Steve Kreuscher, a fifty seven year old school bus driver and amateur artist from Chicago changed his name to

"In God We Trust." The reason why is because it symbolizes the help that God gave him during difficult times.

807. Tobacco has natural sugar in it. Sometimes, however, sugar is added to tobacco manufacturing to create a sweeter smell and taste.

808. The antlers of a moose can be as wide as six feet (1.8 meters) and weigh as much as seventy pounds (thirty one kilograms).

809. In 2004, Barbie and Ken broke up after being together since 1961.

810. In 1947, Austrian tennis player Hans Redl got to the fourth round of the men's singles event at Wimbledon. This was a great achievement given that he only had one arm. He lost one arm during World War II and competed at Wimbledon until 1956.

811. Jackrabbits are actually hares, not rabbits. They can go as fast as forty miles (sixty four kilometers) per hour and jump as high as ten feet (three meters) in the air.

812. There have been seven divorce settlements involving more than one billion dollars. The most recent one was between Jeff Bezos, the Amazon founder, and his wife Mackenzie, which was thirty five billion dollars.

813. Toto, from the "Wizard of Oz," was paid $125 per week. This was more than the Munchkin actors were paid.

814. Located in the southern Pacific Ocean, the Pitcairn Islands are a British overseas territory with a population of about fifty people, most of them descending from nine mutineers of the Bounty ship in 1789. People who are under sixteen years old require a prior clearance before visiting.

815. The law in Indiana stipulates that the coroner has to be elected into office because they vest the authority to arrest sitting sheriffs. The law originates from the twelfth century, because the British king was worried at the time that sheriffs and other officials were becoming too powerful. He chose the coroner to monitor the officials, and in fact, the name coroner came about because coroners represented the crown.

816. Although reindeer and caribou belong to the same species, there are actually differences between them. Caribou, on one

hand, are larger and usually are found in North America and Greenland. On the other hand, reindeer are smaller and can be found in Europe and Asia.

817. One of the worst and most unprofessional fonts is known to be Comic Sans, also known as typeface. However, it is frequently used by and for people with dyslexia because they are able to focus on the individual parts of the words thanks to the irregular shapes in the letters.

818. 300 dairy cows were genetically engineered by Chinese scientists to produce milk that contains nutrients found in human breast milk. This could actually represent a viable alternative to regular infant formula in the future.

819. The Dulle Griet is a bar in Belgium that requires customers to give the bar one of their shoes if they want to drink any of their house beer; the reason behind this is to avoid tourists from stealing their beer glasses. The shoes are then placed in a basket and raised up to the ceiling, which has now become a popular attraction.

820. In theory, a single gram or 0.35 ounces of DNA could hold about 445 exabytes of data, and that's enough capacity to store all the data held by all major tech corporations combined, including Google and Facebook.

821. As of 2018, there are 328 girls in The United States with the name ABCDE according to Vocative.

822. In 2009, a fossil of the Titanoboa was discovered. They were the largest snakes that have ever existed, measuring 9.1 feet (2.8 meters) and weighing 2,495 pounds (1,133 kilograms). Given the warmer climate on Earth fifty eight to sixty million years ago, they were able to reach these fabulous sizes. Today, smaller snakes can be found farther away from the equator, while the larger ones are closer to it.

823. Shy people are more likely to experience anxiety when they're hungover than their extroverted counterparts. The term is called "hangxiety." Professor Celia Morgan of the University of Exeter remarked that shy people should accept the fact that they're introverted and that should help the transition from heavy alcohol consumption.

824. The maximum life expectancy for human beings has constantly increased by three months each year, since 1841, according to a 2002 publication.

825. Millionaire Steve Jobs used to pay only $500 a month in child support to his daughter Lisa.

826. People born in the month of May may have the lowest risk of illness and disease according to a study conducted at Columbia University.

827. Manatees can actually eat a tenth of their body weight in a twenty four hour period, which can be up to 130 pounds (fifty nine kilograms).

828. Located in the McMurdo Dry Valleys of Antarctica, Don Juan Pond is the saltiest body of water in the world, with a salinity level of over 40%. It's an ankle-deep pond in the lowest part of Upper Wright Valley and it's so salty that its waters rarely freeze.

829. Actor, comedian, and writer Stepehn Colbert also exists in the Marvel Universe. He helped defeat a villain with spiderman and also ran for president.

830. One of the most dangerous animals in the world is actually the hippopotamus. Around 500 people a year are killed by hippopotamuses in Africa. These huge animals are capable of running the same speed as humans on land and their jaws are so strong that they could snap a canoe in half.

831. For just under $500, it's possible to buy a child-sized Tesla for your kids. The invention was actually an advertising strategy. Instead of spending money on ads, they make these cars; people buy them and advertise for them by sharing pictures on social media of how cool their kids are.

832. In November of 2016, scientists discovered a spider in southwestern China's Yunnan rainforest that can make itself look like a dangling dried up leaf. The leaf-mimicking spider, as it is named, employs a strategy called masquerading, which consists of pretending to look like something else in order to protect itself.

833. The Amazon and the Rio Negro rivers are two of the largest rivers in the world. At some point they meet, but do not mix;

although they are visually distinct, they both occupy the same body of water. This is due to their different speeds, density, and temperatures.

834. International Redhead Day, also known as "Roodharigendag," is an event held every year in Breda, a small town in Holland, on the first weekend of September. Natural redheads come by the thousands to take part in demonstrations, lectures, and workshops, all centered around having red hair.

835. The largest flying bird in North America is the California condor. Its wingspan can be as wide as ten feet (three meters) from tip to tip and they can fly as high as 15,000 feet (4,500 meters) by catching air currents.

836. Washing machines and chainsaws are very popular among Amish families. In fact, 97% of them use motorized washing machines while 75% of them use chainsaws. In contrast, only 6% of them use tractors for field work.

837. Baseball umpires earn more money annually than referees in the other three Major American Sports leagues with incomes of up to $350,000 a year. NFL referees on the other hand earn up to $70,000 per season, NBA referees earn up to $300,000 annually, and NHL referees earn up to $255,000 annually.

838. It's against the law to wrestle a bear in Alabama.

839. On January 23, 1556, a deadly earthquake occurred in Shaanxi, China, killing an estimated 830,000 people. The magnitude of the quake was approximately 8-8.3. Although it wasn't the strongest tremor on record, it struck in the middle of a densely populated area with poorly constructed buildings and homes, resulting in horrific death tolls.

840. If you take a piece of fresh garlic, cut it in half, put it in a plastic bag, and then put your bare foot in it, you will be able to taste and smell the garlic after an hour. Garlic contains a molecule called "Allicin" which can permeate through the skin of your foot and travel up your bloodstream to the mouth and nose.

841. According Steve Levitt, an economist from the University of Chicago, for every mile (1.6 kilometers) that you walk drunk,

you are eight times more likely to die than if you were to drive a mile drunk.

842. In Scotland, there is an island called "The Island of Discussion" where, historically, those with different arguments and points of view were sent. They would take with them cheese and whiskey to sort out their problems and couldn't leave until they came to a mutual agreement on the subject.

843. During the Wheel of Fortune's 30th anniversary, aired on May 30, thirty year old woman Autumn Erhard won the top prize of one million dollars.

844. Beavers are able to hold their breath underwater for up to fifteen minutes.

845. The opah is the only species of warm-blooded fish on Earth.

846. Originally, hockey pucks were made of cow dung.

847. On August 3, 2016, a neuron out of germanium antimony telluride was created by IBM scientists in Zurich, Switzerland, which replicates a biological neuron. This could actually be the first step for developing an artificial brain.

848. Writer Charles Dickens always wrote and slept while facing north, and he carried around a compass to ensure that he had his directions right. He held the belief that doing so helped increase his creativity.

849. The word "mortgage" comes from the French language meaning "death pledge" which refers to the death of a loan because you amortize a mortgage.

850. Soldiers with mentally low IQs were recruited into the military for the Vietnam War. Unfortunately they were three times more likely to die than any other soldiers.

851. The speed of light travels at 186,000 miles (300,000 kilometers) a second. To put that into perspective, if you were traveling at the speed of light, you would be able to travel around Earth 7.5 times per second.

852. The record for the longest confirmed kill shot in history was done by a Canadian special forces snipe, shooting an IS militant dead from 11,611 feet (3,540 meters) away.

853. The creator of KFC, Colonel Sanders, was fired from a bunch of jobs, including being a lawyer, before he found himself

broke at the age of sixty five, which is when he began his franchise.

854. The basking shark has a liver so big that it weighs almost a third of its total body weight.

855. The largest known prime number ever discovered has 23.2 million digits. The Electric Frontier Foundation offers prizes for anyone who finds record primes. Participants have the opportunity to win over $50,000.

856. If you have the Galaxy Note 7, Samsung Pay allows you to pay for things with just your retina.

857. The Tyrannosaurus Rex was closer to us in time than it was to the Stegosaurus. In fact, the Stegosaurus was already a fossil by the time the T-Rex roamed the Earth.

858. Chinsekikan is a museum located in Chichibu, Japan, that has almost 2,000 rocks that resemble human faces. The museum's name means "hall of curious rocks."

859. Potato chips cause significantly more weight gain in people than most other foods, according to a 2011 Harvard study.

860. The University of Oregon's mascot, known as the Oregon duck, is based on Disney's Donald Duck. A special license agreement between the school and the company was signed.

861. Twenty of the twenty four men who traveled to the moon on Apollo 8 and Apollo 10 through seventeen missions were Boy Scouts. This includes eleven of the twelve moonwalkers and all three members of the Apollo 13 crew.

862. Any plane that the president of the United States happens to be traveling on at a particular time is given the name Air Force One. Likewise, the Army aircraft that the president is traveling on is called Army One while the helicopter is called Marine One.

863. After graduating from high school at the age of sixteen, Jessica Alba was already a successful actress.

864. Susan Bennett, a voice actor and former backup singer for Roy Orbison, is the female voice of the original Siri. A company called "ScanSoft" hired her to record gibberish. Technicians then took those recordings and combined them to form sentences and phrases, which ended up on all those devices.

865. Ted Bundy, a notorious serial killer, shockingly served as the assistant director of the Seattle Crime Prevention Advisory Commission. He was even the author of a pamphlet instructing women on rape prevention.

866. The Dunning-Kruger Effect is a cognitive bias where smart people underestimate themselves while ignorant people think they are brilliant. In other words, the highly-skilled assume that things that they find easy are also easy for others, while the unskilled are so incompetent that they can't even recognize their own stupidity.

867. Hummingbirds can only be found in the Western hemisphere. About half of them live around the Equator, while 5% live in the north of Mexico, and about two dozen species live in the United States and Canada.

868. Mike Kroeger named his band Nickelback after his cashier experience at a Starbucks. Many customers used to pay $1.50 for a coffee that cost $1.45, so he always had to give them a nickel back.

869. In some China subway stations, there are people who are employed to shove passengers into crowded trains so the doors can shut as quickly as possible avoiding delays.

870. The land that served as the headquarters of the Ku Klux Klan in Atlanta, Georgia, was bought by the Catholic Church. They turned it into a church called the Cathedral of Christ the King.

871. Tetris was the first video game ever to be played in space. Aleksandr A. Serobrov, a Russian cosmonaut, brought a Game Boy along during a 1993 space mission, and he played Tetris on it.

872. Dysania is a term used to describe the difficulty of waking up and getting out of bed in the morning.

873. Violet Jessop worked as a ship nurse on the Britannic, the Olympic, and the Titanic. The Olympic collided with a warship and nearly sank. The Titanic hit an iceberg and sank. And the Britannic hit an underwater mine and sank. Yet Violet survived all three.

874. There is a service dog named Opal that not only leads her blind owner around, but she has also become a guide dog to

the family's previous guide dog, Edward. Edward had taken care of the owner for six years, but he had his eyes removed after developing cataracts.

875. In 2014, the number one cause of death in the United States according to the Center of Disease Control and Prevention was heart disease with over 600,000 deaths, followed by cancer, with 591,000.

876. To go into hypovolemic shock, it only takes the loss of 20% of your blood. The condition leads to major organ failure because the heart loses the pressure it needs to circulate blood.

877. Dr. Timothy Clarke Smith, of Vermont, was afraid of being buried alive, so he left precise instructions to build a window looking down into his coffin. He is currently buried in Evergreen Cemetery with a headstone that has a 1.18 foot (thirty centimeter) glass window that is still there today.

878. The University of Washington Huskies have a live mascot, but it isn't a husky, it's really an Alaskan malamute they've named Dubs II.

879. In Japan, crows have mastered a new method of cracking nuts. They drop the nuts on the street, wait for a car to run over them, and then retrieve the nuts when they crack.

880. The toothpick capital of the world is considered to be Strong, in Maine. Up until 2003, they manufactured 90% of the US supply of toothpicks, producing twenty million toothpicks a day.

881. In Boston, there is a Museum of Bad Art. It is the world's only museum that is entirely dedicated to bad art in all of its forms.

882. In 1976, Ronald Wayne designed the very first Apple computer logo; he is considered by many people to be the third co-founder of the company. The logo featured Sir Isaac Newton sitting under a tree just as an apple is about to hit him on the head.

883. Tornadoes can occur on the surface of the sun. In September of 2015, NASA captured on film a giant swirling plume of superheated plasma churned above the surface of the sun for about forty hours. It was five million degrees Fahrenheit (2.7 million degrees Celsius).

884. In the 1800's, one of the first ever iron maidens was found in a castle in Nuremberg, Germany. It is a device of torture where the person is put inside a sarcophagus with spikes on the inner surface. When the doors were closed, the spikes would puncture several organs, including their eyes, but not deep enough to kill them, just deep enough that they would bleed to death over several hours.

885. One of the hardest plants to grow in the world is wasabi. In order to be cultivated well, it needs cold pure running water. In addition to that, it takes over a year for it to mature. If there is too much humidity or the wrong nutrient composition, the entire crop will be completely wiped out.

886. Bob Ross made the "Joy of Painting" series completely for free and only made money from his art supply store.

887. The body of a man and a bear were found dead next to one another in 1883 with the area around them trashed. It's believed that the both of them fought till the death.

888. In South Korea, there is a fake prison where stressed-out business people and students check themselves into in order to relax and find relief. There, mobile phones or clocks are not allowed and it's also forbidden to talk to other inmates. Their menu is rice porridge for breakfast and a steamed sweet potato with a banana milkshake for dinner.

889. On August 25, 2014, Alexandru Duru achieved the farthest flight on a hoverboard in Quebec, Canada, which was 905 feet (276 meters).

890. "Gitumo" is a form of meditation implemented by Tibetan nuns, which can actually change their core body temperatures. A team of researchers once recorded the internal temperature of the nuns in the freezing cold temperatures of the Himalayas, using special temperature measurements and, incredibly, the nuns were able to increase their core body temperature up to almost 101 degrees Fahrenheit (thirty eight degrees Celsius).

891. After banning alcohol in the Indian village of Marottichal, residents began playing chess as a substitute for drinking. The village is now known as Chess Village due to its near 100% chess literacy.

892. After the incident where a shoe was thrown by a journalist at George W. Bush during his last visit to Iraq, the town of Tikrit in Iraq erected a six foot (two meter tall) monument to the shoe.

893. Almost half of the world's population is at risk for malaria, according to the World Health Organization. In 2015, for example, there were about 212 million malaria cases and approximately 429,000 deaths. Out of those, 90% of malaria cases and 92% of malaria deaths were found in sub-Saharan Africa.

894. In the 19th century, Americans intentionally filled their parks with squirrels for entertainment purposes. Before that, squirrels were hardly found outside of forests.

895. Fainting goats exist. There is even a Fainting Goat Festival that is held in Tennessee. These goats are born with a condition called "myotonia congenital," which causes their muscles to tense up for ten to twenty seconds whenever they are spooked, which can cause them to easily faint.

896. According to a study published by the Journal of Transportation, people who are bicycling are in the best mood compared to any other means of transportation.

897. We are now living at a time that's closer to when the Jetsons was set (2062), than when it originally aired (1962).

898. The longest coastline in the United States belongs to Alaska at 6,640 miles (10,683 kilometers) long.

899. Michael Jackson wanted to make a Harry Potter musical, but author J.K. Rowling turned down the offer as she later confessed on Oprah Winfrey.

900. The word dinosaur was invented in 1842 by Richard Owen. It comes from the ancient Greek words "deinos," meaning fearfully-great, and "sauros," meaning lizard.

901. Richard Nixon appeared on the cover of Time Magazine fifty five times, more than any other individual.

902. Actress Lucille Ball from the hit show "I Love Lucy" found out that she was pregnant during season two of the show. CBS agreed to write her pregnancy into the show, but the network

considered that the word pregnant was too vulgar, so they used instead the word expecting.

903. In 2010, a study revealed that men who wear red appear more attractive to women. Red appeared to signify higher status and power which lead to increased attraction.

904. The only continent that doesn't have rabies according to the World Health Organization is the Antarctic. About 95% of human deaths that occur in Africa and Asia are actually caused by rabies.

905. An average of $1,100 per year is spent by Americans on clothes for themselves.

906. After the release of the 1996 horror movie "Scream," Caller ID tripled in the United States. The film was about a killer who would anonymously call his victims before attacking them.

907. Mexico's official legal name is the United Mexican States, a name that even today is still used by the country's government.

908. There is a species of orchid that looks pretty much like a monkey. It only grows at high elevations, in certain mountainous areas of Ecuador, Colombia, and Peru.

909. The Mimic octopus lives in the waters off the Asian coast in the Southeast. It can blend with its environment by changing its color, and it can also copy the physical characteristics and movements of other aquatic animals. It manipulates its body and tentacles to look and move like snakes, eels, stingrays, jellyfish, starfish, and other creatures.

910. Actor Christian Bale had to lose sixty three pounds (twenty nine kilograms) for his role in "The Machinist." His daily diet consisted of one can of tuna, an apple, black coffee, and water.

911. If you earn just $32,000 per year, that puts you in the top 1% of income earners in the world.

912. There are coffin clubs intended for senior citizens where they get together and build their own customized coffins.

913. Men have a tendency of being more emotionally affected than women with regard to relationship issues, it's just that they are better at hiding it.

914. Mother Teresa was canonized on September 4, 2016, by Pope Francis, officially making her Saint Teresa. Her

canonization happened almost twenty years after her death, in 1997.

915. In China, a puppy was taught to smoke cigarettes by his owner, a twenty three year old chef named Zeng Ziguang. The man would blow smoke in his face to get him used to the smell and used treats to get him to hold the cigarette in his mouth. After a month, the puppy was smoking a pack a day.

916. While flying, albatross are able to sleep. They do this to avoid predators like whales and sharks.

917. If somebody is considered unfit to serve in the US Military, they are given a 4F classification. This term came about a long time ago during the American Civil War and it literally meant the person lacked the four front teeth, which were necessary to open packs of gunpowder. Some young able-bodied men would avoid service by pulling out their front teeth.

918. Brent and Wayne Gretzky hold the record for most points in the NHL by a pair of brothers. They totaled 2,861 points with Brent scoring four of those points and Wayne scoring the other 2,857.

919. The only IRS revenue officer to ever be killed while in duty was Michael Dillon. In 1983, he went to collect a sum of $500 from a former service employee on behalf of the IRS. Unfortunately, he was shot three times by the resident with an M-1 rifle and was killed instantly.

920. Located in a small town just north of Munich, the Von Schesteffan Brewery has been brewing beer uninterruptedly for almost a thousand years, withstanding four fires, three plagues, and a major earthquake.

921. In some states it is against the law to take a selfie at the voting booth. People can be fined or even face jail time if doing so.

922. Before even thinking of starting an acting career, Idris Elba used to be a drug dealer. He would sell marijuana while he was a bouncer at the popular club Carolines. Celebrities who went regularly to the nightclub, like D.L. Hughley and Dave Chappelle, simply knew him as the doorman.

923. It's possible to see coral reefs and underwater sea life by using Google Maps.

924. Horses are physically unable to vomit. They have a number of physiological features that ensure that any food they ingest takes a one-way trip. They have, for example, a much lower esophageal sphincter that is much stronger than in other animals, making it nearly impossible to open that valve under backward pressure from the stomach.

925. A device that can translate the vocalizations of animals into something that we can understand is being developed by scientists through the use of artificial intelligence. After studying and gathering data from prairie dogs for thirty years, scientists discovered that they have their own language system.

926. In 2012, wine producer Ian Hutcheon launched the world's first meteorite-aged wine at his Tremonte Vineyard in the Cachapoal Valley, in Chile. It's a Cabernet Sauvignon called Meteorite that was aged with a 4.5 billion year old meteorite from the asteroid belt between Mars and Jupiter.

927. In La Crosse, Kansas, there is a museum dedicated to barbed wire.

928. To prevent rigor mortis, beef carcasses are given electrical stimulation before they are slaughtered and skinned.

929. There was an island called "Sandy Island" that was located between New Caledonia and Australia according to maps for over a hundred years. That was until a team of scientists went to look at it in 2012 only to find out it doesn't exist.

930. Since 2003, happy hour has been illegal in the Republic of Ireland according to their Intoxicating Liquor Act.

931. In Sicily, Italy, five high school students and their teacher created a prototype of a vending machine that turns plastic recyclables into phone cases. It grinds down the plastics into tiny pellets which are then melted and used to create 3D printed phone cases. The project was intended to encourage young people to recycle more.

932. A hand-written book known as the Voynich Manuscript has 246 pages and many illustrations in approximately 170 thousand characters. Strangely, the script in the book is completely unknown and illegible, so no one has ever been able to read or decipher it.

933. At the federal level, the United States does not have an official language. However, English is considered the official language in thirty two states.

934. In 1952, the presidency of Israel was actually offered to Albert Einstein, but he politely turned down the offer.

935. Edward Nigma or E. Nigma was Riddler's real name in the Batman stories. He also has some other aliases such as the Prince of Puzzlers, the Crown Prince of Conundrums, and the Wizard of Quiz.

936. In 1997, a man in Frankfurt, Germany, went to the police to report his car stolen. Twenty years later, the car was tracked down by the police, finding out that the man just forgot where he parked it, and he just assumed it was stolen.

937. The only musician in history to be inducted into the Rock and Roll Hall of Fame three times is legendary guitarist Eric Clapton. The first time was in 1992, when he was a member of The Yardbirds. The second was in 1993, when Cream was inducted. And the third time was in 2000, when he was inducted as a solo artist.

938. In 2012, a cat fell from a nineteen-story window in Boston and incredibly survived. The animal literally only walked away with a bruised chest.

939. When the Confederate Army was running out of gunpowder, bat's poop was the solution. Bat guano's high nitrate content provided a key ingredient for the production of gunpowder.

940. French fries were partly made popular in America by Thomas Jefferson. He came back from France with instructions for making "Pommes de terre frites a cru en petites tranches" which means raw potatoes that are cut into small pieces and deep-fried. Although French fries didn't become popular until the twentieth century, the recipe he wrote down is fifty years older than early French-fry entries on cookbooks.

941. All countries worldwide use the Gregorian calendar, except for Ethiopia, Iran, and Afghanistan.

942. There is a fifty six feet (seventeen meter) glass structure shaped like a giant high heel shoe built in Chiayi, Taiwan. The structure is a tourist attraction, but it's also used as a wedding

hall. It was built in honor of women who suffered from arsenic poisoning from well water that caused gangrene, a condition sometimes known as black feet disease.

943. Under Hitler, Nazi Germany guillotined about as many people as those who were executed using the same method during the French Revolution.

944. There is a sixty acre forest near Walt Disney World which has the largest hidden Mickey Mouse; the forest has over 50,000 pine trees.

945. The world's first cyborg artist is a man named Neil Harbisson. He has an antenna implanted in his skull, which allows him to hear colors and see sounds. He can also connect to nearby devices via Bluetooth and Wi-Fi.

946. There is a rare species of shark known as the Megamouth shark, which we have only sixty records of since their discovery in 1976.

947. Musa Velutina is a type of banana. They are pink and peel themselves when ripe. Although they are often grown as ornamental, they are still edible; the flesh is soft and sweet, but the seeds are quite hard and can even chip a tooth.

948. The Indian Ocean earthquake and tsunami of 2004 was so powerful that it caused the entire planet to vibrate as much as 0.39 inches (one centimeter). It also distantly triggered earthquakes on the other side of Earth, as far as in Alaska. Additionally, it was the longest lasting earthquake ever recorded with a duration between eight and ten minutes.

949. Bill Gates got married on the Hawaiian island of Lanai. To ensure his privacy, he rented every room at the hotel he was staying at (up to 250 rooms), and chartered every helicopter close-by.

950. Close to $1 billion worth of gift cards are unused every year according to the advisory company CEB TowerGroup.

951. In 1956, the Canadian Army put on an exhibition to show a bazooka type of weapon during a fair. The testing resulted in a bad incident, so they didn't use it any more.

952. In 2017, a plot to steal legendary racing pioneer Enzo Ferrari's body from a cemetery was stopped by the Italian police. The

group of thieves planned to ask for money in exchange for the body. Ferrari died in 1988 at ninety years old.

953. There is an unnamed species of octopus that is so cute that scientists are pushing to have it named "Opisthoteuthis Adorabilis."

954. There is a condition called "situs inversus" where one in about every 8,500 people is born with their organs in their chest and abdomen in perfect mirror image reversal of their normal positioning. These people have their hearts on the right and liver and spleen on the left.

955. "Momentary Ink" is a company that prints temporary tailor-made tattoo designs, lasting three to ten days. The idea is that you try it out before you really commit to one.

956. In 2016, a report from the US News & World Report showed that only 18% of American drivers know how to operate a stick shift, and only about 5% of cars sold in the United States today come with a stick shift.

957. In 1976, a group of people created the National Fancy Rat Society, with the aim to promote the rat as a pet and an exhibition animal.

958. As per the Center for Disease Control and Prevention ,30,700 Americans lost their lives to alcohol related causes in 2014, a number that's higher than the combined total deaths that resulted from heroin and prescription pain medication overdoses.

959. Chinchillas (a type of rodent) don't suffer from fleas. Their fur is so thick and soft that fleas will suffocate if they try to live in it.

960. When photosynthesis occurs in oceans, as when algae turn sunlight into energy, it makes a ping sound. Scientists believe that these sounds could act as a sort of stethoscope when checking for health of a coral reef.

961. By combining the sound of an elephant call with a car driving on wet pavement, sound designer Ben Burtt created the distinctive sound for the TIE fighter from the "Star Wars" movies. According to the book "The Sounds of Star Wars," the sound of the engine was supposed to imitate the German

junker bombers that would use sirens to scare civilians during raids.

962. In China, there are some restaurants that lace their foods with opiates to keep customers coming back.

963. The Basenji is a dog breed that doesn't have the ability to bark, but instead it can produce a yodeling howl sound. It's a small to medium sized, square-shaped dog that is believed to be bred intentionally without the ability to bark.

964. Every fourteen days, a different language dies, according to National Geographic. In addition, half of the roughly 7,000 languages spoken on earth will most likely disappear in the next century because more communities are starting to put aside their native tongues in favor of Mandarin, English, and Spanish.

965. The whiptail lizard is the only all-female species as the males are completely extinct. Despite that, they are not hermaphroditic; the females actually lay and hatch from unfertilized eggs.

966. According to a study conducted at the University of Central Florida, people who have had bad or abusive bosses in the past will make themselves into a better boss when the time comes.

967. A man with a Liverpool FC tattoo on his leg with the club motto "you'll never walk alone" had his lower leg amputated after a combat injury in Afghanistan. The surgery unknowingly cut his tattoo to read "you'll never walk." Luckily, the man got a prosthetic leg and now even runs marathons.

968. In 1620, the colonists aboard the Mayflower decided to settle at Plymouth after sixty four days at sea because they ran out of beer on the ship. Their beer was a relatively low alcoholic formula and was drunk because it was boiled purer than regular water.

969. In 1931, an eleven year old named Wilbur Brink was playing in his front yard when he was suddenly hit by a stray tire flying out that instantly killed him. The tire came from a wreck involving race driver Billy Arnold who was racing at a spot across the street.

970. Most planets have been named after Greek mythology

characters. Uranus' moons on the contrary have been named after characters in Shakespeare's plays, such as Umbriel, Cordelia, and Ariel.

971. Robert Landsburg was an American photographer who on May 18, 1980, documented the eruption of Mt. Saint Helens. It dawned on him that he couldn't outrun the clouds of volcanic ash that were coming towards him, so he chose to preserve his record by rewinding the film, enclosing his equipment in its proper case, and then laying his body over the case to protect it. Seventeen days later, he was found dead, but his work was preserved, and it was used by geologists to study key details of the eruption.

972. Bradley Cooper's dream as a child was to train as a ninja and wanted his father to send him to Japan so he could learn to become one.

973. According to the University of Southern Queensland, facial hair can block up to 95% of the sun's harmful UV rays, protecting you from cancer.

974. In 2017, Leonardo da Vinci's Salvator Mundi was sold for $450 million dollars at an auction to a prince from Abu Dhabi, becoming the most expensive painting ever sold.

975. A man named Roger Tullgren from Sweden was given benefits for his disability when his obsession with heavy metal music was officially declared as an addiction.

976. A Polish doctor created a fake Typhus epidemic in World War II which prevented the Nazis from sending 8,000 Jews to concentration camps as they had phobias about hygiene.

977. There is a weight loss competition in Dubai called the "Your Child In Gold." The competition aims to fight early aged obesity and the winner receives eighty eight pounds (forty kilograms) in gold.

978. Koumpounophobia is the fear of buttons. Although it is differently manifested in sufferers, some people feel that buttons are dirty and some are afraid of the texture of certain buttons.

979. Over 2,500 species of fish are found in the Amazon basin. That is more than the ones found in the entire Atlantic Ocean.

980. According to PhD candidate Alexis Noel, from the Georgia

Institute of Technology, frogs can change the viscosity of their saliva in a fraction of a second. By withdrawing their eyeballs inside of their heads, frogs help create the pressure needed to change the saliva.

981. The honey bee has microscopic short hairs on its eyes called "settey." They help with navigation by catching the wind to help them figure out direction and speed while traveling.

982. Even though NBA superstar LeBron James is left-handed, he shoots the ball with his right hand. Similarly, Hall of Famer Larry Bird of the Boston Celtics was a player who was left-handed, but he shot the ball with the right.

983. Javelins are permitted on Delta Air Lines, except for flights departing from or landing in Amsterdam in the Netherlands, or Dublin in Ireland.

984. A Chinese man bought and raised two puppies, taking care of them despite their frequent killing and eating of chickens. He later realized that they were bears.

985. A type of tumor known as "teratoma" can grow hair, teeth, organs, and limbs. Scientists are still uncertain why they form.

986. Baby kangaroos or joeys can be as small as a grain of rice or as big as a bee at birth.

987. Saudi Arabia's Grand Mufti, Abdul Aziz Al Sheikh, has banned chess in Islam, as it's believed to be a form of gambling and a waste of time and money. He also claimed that it causes hatred and enmity between the players.

988. Once a terminal patient was pronounced dead, but brain activity continued for about ten minutes. Doctors from the University of Western Ontario observed the unusual event and had no explanation for it.

989. The only American president with a Ph.D. was President Woodrow Wilson.

990. McDonald's takes approximately 7% of all potatoes grown in the United States and turns them into french fries.

991. Rabbits can die of fright. Loud sounds such as dogs barking, loud music, or screaming can cause a heart attack, putting a rabbit into shock and causing sudden death.

992. A man named Seth Putnam once wrote a song about how

stupid being in a coma was. Shortly after he wrote it he went into a coma. When he woke up afterwards and was asked how it felt, he responded: "Being in a coma was just as stupid as I wrote it was."

993. In Devon, UK, there is a nightclub that gave out free lollipops to its clubbers to reduce late-night rowdiness. They hoped that drunken clubbers would be busy sucking the lollipops, hence they wouldn't shout or cause any trouble. It worked.

994. The giant red spot on Jupiter is actually a storm. It has been going on for around 150 years and is twice as wide as Earth. On Earth, the largest and most powerful hurricanes ever recorded spanned over 1,000 miles (1,600 kilometers) across with wind speeds of up to 200 miles (322 kilometers) per hour. The giant red spot, however, has wind speeds twice as fast.

995. Chips have a vanishing caloric density that tricks our tongue and brain into thinking that we haven't actually eaten anything. This is why it's so easy to eat a full bag of them without even noticing.

996. Barn owls are usually monogamous birds. However, a study performed by the University of Lausanne showed that during a year where the bird couples don't have many babies, they may divorce each other and move on to a new mate. The male is often the one to stay at the original breeding ground.

997. A hundred cats were unleashed into an Ikea in England in 2010, just so they could see what would happen.

998. US former president John Quincy Adams had an alligator as a pet. He used to keep it in the bathtub in the East Room of the White House.

999. When senior crayon maker at Crayola Emerson Moser retired after working for thirty seven years at the company, he made an announcement that he was in fact colorblind.

1000. In 1936, the world's largest book called "The Golden Book of Cleveland" suddenly disappeared during some time in Cleveland, Ohio. The book measured 6.88 feet (2.1 meters) by 4.92 feet (1.5 meters) by 3.28 feet (one meter) thick, and weighed 4,993 pounds (2,267 kilograms). To put that into perspective, that's about the same size as a queen size bed.

1001. Some of the world's oldest sunglasses were created by the Eskimo or Inuit of the Arctic on North Baffin Island, in northern Canada. Also referred to as snow goggles, they were made out of bone, leather, or wood, with small slits to see through; they were designed to protect the eyes from snow-blindness produced by the sun.

1002. The tallest mountain on the African continent is Mount Kilimanjaro. It is also the highest free-standing mountain in the world.

1003. When a cheetah runs at full sprint, it actually spends more time flying than in contact with the ground.

1004. When the CEO of Sesame Street Gery Knell was asked if Ernie and Bert were gay he responded: "they're not gay, they're not straight, they don't exist below the waist."

1005. Elvis Presley once gave his limo driver a gift of the exact same limo that he had been driving Elvis in.

1006. Located in Oak Bluffs, on Martha's Vineyard, the Flying Horses Carousel is the oldest carousel in the United States. It was built in 1876 and it's still running. It is one of the twenty surviving carousels that include a ring machine and people who grab the ring get a free ride.

1007. Over 500,000 pieces of debris orbit Earth, traveling at speeds up to 17,489 miles (28,163 kilometers) per hour. From these intense speeds, even the tiniest chip of paint has actually caused damages to space crafts.

1008. A diaper equipped with a waterproof baby wipe holding compartment was actually invented by actress Jamie Lee Curtis. Her experience and time spent at taking care of children made her think that the conventional diaper system could use some tweaking.

1009. Every single night orangutans build a brand new nest to sleep. They are made from leaves, branches, and sticks, and are thirty nine feet (twelve meters) off the ground. They have to be sturdy, as the average orangutan weighs eighty four pounds (thirty eight kilograms). Although it is a lot of work to do every day, these animals rarely reuse or even improve an old one, opting instead to start from zero.

1010. In Honolulu, Hawaii, stealing spam is starting to be considered a form of organized crime, as the number of cases has greatly increased in the last years.

1011. They are currently developing a new kind of cheerleading called Paracheer. The idea is that athletic teams made up of individuals both with and without disabilities will perform routines that involve dancing, jumping, and creative stunts.

1012. The larvae of the Middle Eastern epomis beetle socialize in killing frogs, salamanders, and other amphibians that try to eat them. They lure in their prey and encourage them to approach; they attack by striking with double-hooked jaws hanging on and then eat the prey alive.

1013. The mantis shrimp can punch fifty times during a blink of an eye, with a speed equal to a bullet. In fact, a blow from a mantis shrimp can easily break through the shell of a crab or mollusk.

1014. Sushi is actually meant to be eaten with your hands and sashimi with chopsticks.

1015. In 2014, a study done by St. Michael's Hospital on homeless men revealed that almost half of them have suffered from at least one traumatic brain injury in their life. In 87% of the cases, those injuries occurred before they lost their homes.

1016. When staring at a bright light such as the sun or a strong light bulb, 7% of the people will experience a sneeze reflex. Of that 7%, 94% of them will be Caucasian.

1017. China is actually monitoring and testing their sewage for traces of drugs that are excreted through urine. According to officials, a drug manufacturer was already caught and arrested by using this technique.

1018. The North Pole hosts the coldest marathon on Earth every year. Runners have to dress in thermal layers, windproof pants, and goggles due to the extreme temperatures, which are usually below zero when they run the twenty six miles (forty two kilometers).

1019. The only American president to ever receive a patent was President Abraham Lincoln, on May 22, 1849. The patent was issued for a device that lifts boats over shoals; however, the invention was never manufactured.

1020. There is a sealed wine bottle that dates back to between 325 and 350 A.D., during the Ancient Roman period, called the "Speyer." It was found when archeologists were excavating a fourth-century nobleman's tomb. It is considered the oldest-known bottle of wine in the world.

1021. Due to the heavy dust particles that block out most of the sun's light, sunsets on Mars are blue instead of red. However, the blue light pushes through the atmosphere better than the red or yellow colors, and is much more visible.

1022. In February 2017, 104 satellites on a single mission were successfully launched by India from the Sriharikota Space Center in South India, beating the previous record of only thirty-seven satellites launched by Russia in 2014.

1023. Glycyrrhizin is a substance contained in licorice root that is about fifty times sweeter than sugar.

1024. People in North America take less time for vacation, work more, and retire later than other industrialised countries.

1025. Approximately 40% of Vietnamese people share the same last name, with Nguyen being the most popular last name, while the top fourteen most popular names make up 90% of the population. Compared to the United States, the top fourteen last names in the country only makeup fewer than 6%.

1026. In Japan, a typhoon turbine has been developed by inventor Atsushi Shimizu. It can withstand typhoon-force winds and convert the energy into electricity. In fact, one typhoon could power all of Japan for fifty years.

1027. As an adaptation mechanism to dry environments, roadrunners do not need to drink water. Instead they get all of the moisture they need from their food. They're also known to kill and eat rattlesnakes.

1028. Taller people have more cells in their bodies than shorter people; in consequence, they are at a greater risk to be diagnosed with cancer as more mutations in the cells can occur.

1029. The United States Postal Service handles approximately 47% of the world's mail volume.

1030. A study done by Biology Letters concluded that the duration of time it takes for an animal to yawn predicts the size of its brain and the number of neurons in its cortex. The longer the yawn is, the bigger the brain is.

1031. According to the Guinness World Records, on June 17, 1998, a man from the United Kingdom named John Evan set a world record in Los Angeles by balancing eighteen empty beer kegs on his head for ten seconds.

1032. Walking corpse syndrome or Cotard syndrome is a mental disorder where patients experience delusions that they are dead, don't exist, are putrefying, or have lost their vital organs.

1033. In Thailand, rats are considered a delicacy.

1034. Disposable diapers in Norway are the cheapest in all of Europe. In fact, many Russians smuggle them over the northern border.

1035. When General Motors revealed the Camaro name in 1966, Automotive Press asked Chevrolet product managers what a Camaro was. The answer was: "it's a small vicious animal that eats mustangs."

1036. Since 2005, people in Estonia have been able to vote via the Internet.

1037. The average family household loses up to sixty socks every year.

1038. The "335 Years War" is considered the longest war ever recorded in human history. It happened between 1651 and 1986, and it involved the Isles of Scilly and the Netherlands. There were however no deaths or injuries, and not even one shot was fired.

1039. The winter was so cold in 2015 that it caused some parts of Niagara Falls to freeze, something that hasn't happened in decades.

1040. According to the provincial government in Alberta, Canada, the region has been rat-free for more than fifty years. Even though it's known that rodents do enter through trucks, trains, and on foot, they are almost always alone; hence they cannot breed to create more.

1041. In Italy, it's forbidden to leave towels, chairs, or sun umbrellas overnight to save a spot on a busy beach. Officers will take what you left behind and fine you about $220 to get your property back.

1042. Frane Selak is considered as the world's luckiest man. Throughout his life, he survived a train crash that killed seventeen, he was blown out of a plane that killed nineteen, and survived a bus accident at the age of four. He has also been in two car explosions, was hit by a bus, and had a close call with a truck. In 2003 he went on to win the lottery.

1043. Actress Candace Bergen didn't receive a single penny from her father while his ventriloquist dummy got $10,000. In reference to the dummy, he said: "The dummy had been my constant companion from whom I have never been separated, even for a day."

1044. Hopeful contestants are not allowed to compete on "Wheel of Fortune" or "Jeopardy!" if they have already competed on any other national game show.

1045. Polar bears have the unique ability to ingest and store very high amounts of vitamin A. The amount is so high, that if you ate a polar bear's liver, it's likely that you could die from vitamin A poisoning, also known as hypervitaminosis A.

1046. Snowflake is the only known albino gorilla. He was born in the wild but in 1966, he was caught by villagers and lived in the Barcelona Zoo until he died of skin cancer in 2003. Spanish researchers think that Snowflake was the result of inbreeding between an uncle and a niece.

1047. On January 13, 1996, nine year old Amber Hagerman was kidnapped and murdered, and the killer was never found. The Amber Alert that is put out when a child goes missing actually came about after this sad event. It alerts local broadcasters and law enforcement to come together to get information out quickly following a child's abduction. It's known nationwide as an Amber Alert, which stands for America's Missing Broadcast Emergency Response.

1048. Even though it is very unusual, it is possible to get heart cancer. At the Mayo Clinic, one case of heart cancer is treated every year.

1049. In order to capture scent particles, snakes and lizards flick their tongues in the air. This basically means that they smell with their tongues.

1050. A live alligator was once thrown into a Wendy's drive-thru window by a man in Jupiter, Florida, after the server handed over his drink. The man confessed to picking up the 3.5 feet (1.07 meter) long gator from the side of the road; he was charged with aggravated assault, unlawful possession, and transportation of an alligator.

1051. In the 1500's, King Frances the first of France bought the Mona Lisa from Renaissance artist Leonardo de Vinci.

1052. During summer, Alaska has as much as twenty hours of sunshine per day. This allows them to grow vegetables of gigantic proportions, like 137 pound (sixty two kilogram) cabbages, sixty four (twenty-nine kilogram) cantaloupes, and thirty five pound (sixteen kilogram) broccoli.

1053. Iceland has about 1,300 different types of insects, but no mosquitoes at all. However, the neighboring countries of Greenland, Scotland, and Denmark all have mosquitoes.

1054. The Soviets thought that women were the best to fit in sniper duties as they need to be patient, careful, and deliberate. They would also avoid hand to hand combat and need higher levels of aerobic conditioning than other troops.

1055. When Barack Obama visited Cuba in March, 2016, he became the first US President to do so in eighty eight years. Calvin Coolidge was the last president to make the trip in 1928.

1056. "Rigatoni con la pajata" is a classic Roman dish consisting of the intestines of an unweaned calf that was only fed on its mother's milk. The intestines become a thick and creamy cheese-like sauce after they are cooked, which is then served with tomato sauce and rigatoni.

1057. In 1998, construction worker Travis Bogumill was accidentally shot with a nail gun, causing a 3.25 inch (8.25 centimeter) nail to go right into his skull, which got stuck in the area of the brain that usually involves processing math. After removing the nail, he was completely fine, except his math skills weren't what they used to be.

1058. To produce a USD $100 bill, it only costs 14.3 cents. However, it costs over 1.43 cents to make every penny. This is the reason why other major countries have already eliminated pennies altogether.

1059. In Ancient Sparta, there was a training program called "Agoge" that was mandatory for all male citizens, except for the firstborns of the ruling houses. Some of the training consisted of being underfed to encourage stealing; if the students were caught however, they would be punished. The reason behind this was that their master wanted them to become fit soldiers, not fat ones.

1060. According to different studies conducted by the Global Commission on Aging at the Transamerica Center for Retirement Studies, traveling brings great benefits to your mind and body, as it promotes brain health and decreases your risk of heart attack and depression.

1061. There is a syndrome where people sneeze when they look at the sun. It's called a photic sneeze reflex, also known as autosomal dominant compelling helio-ophthalmic outburst syndrome. The abbreviation is "ADCHOO."

1062. "Radaranges" was the name originally given to microwave ovens. The invention is generally credited to American engineer Percy Spencer, who created it after World War II from radar technology developed during the war. It was first sold in 1946.

1063. The first and largest stadium ever built in Ancient Rome was "The Circus Maximus," which accommodated 150,000 people. However, the massive stadium decayed and quarried off for materials during the sixth century. Today it's a park in Rome.

1064. Kamikatsu, a small Japanese town, has been trying since 2003 to become the country's first zero-waste community. They already recycle 80% of their waste and currently have thirty-four different recycling categories.

1065. In 2016, garlic flavored black Doritos were introduced in Japan, right before Halloween. The bag is black and it features a haunted house, bats, and a Dracula graphic.

1066. "Ed, Edd, Eddy" was the last major cartoon show to utilize traditional animation techniques before CGI was introduced in subsequent shows.

1067. The human tongue has between 2,000 and 4,000 taste buds. They contain sensory cells that renew themselves every seven days.

1068. The political opponents of Andrew Jackson used to refer to him as a jackass, so he decided to adopt the name and use it as his campaign symbol. Eventually, it became the symbol of the entire Democratic Party in America.

1069. For the construction of the USS New York, in 2005, approximately 6.8 tons of steel was used from the rubble of the World Trade Center towers.

1070. In 2012, a chicken McNugget was sold on eBay by a woman named Rebecca Spiggot, from Dakota City. She sold it for eight thousand dollars, simply because it looked like George Washington.

1071. There are four personal pronouns in the word USHER; he, she, her, and us.

1072. Based on reports done by the US Bureau of Labor Statistics, a $100,000 a year salary in 1950 is equivalent to more than $1 million salary in 2019 when adjusted for inflation.

1073. The word with the most meanings in the English language according to the Guinness World Records is the verb "set." The Second Edition of the Oxford English dictionary published in 1989 shows 430 senses listed in it. The word has the longest entry in the dictionary with 60,000 words, or 236,000 characters.

1074. In 2014, the world record for the highest altitude free fall jump was set by American computer scientist Alan Eustace, even though he was in his late 50's. He fell from an altitude of 25.7 miles (41.4 kilometers), reaching speeds of 821.5 miles (1,323 kilometers) per hour. The total descent lasted for four minutes and twenty seven seconds.

1075. The "Georgium Sidus" was the name originally given to planet Uranus, after King George, the third of England. The name Uranus was proposed by German astronomer Johann Elert Bode and it did not become the common name until 1850.

1076. Andorra does not have an active military, so every citizen in the country should own a rifle by law. In fact, the police force will offer a firearm to citizens if it's needed.

1077. The one ounce gold American Eagle coin is legal tender; they are worth $1,295 US dollars each. The one ounce silver American Eagle coin is the only silver bullion coin that is approved as legal tender and is worth about $17.50 US each.

1078. People in Thailand text each other "555" instead of "hahaha" because the number five is pronounced the same way as "ha."

1079. The word emoji is the Japanese term for picture characters. They were created out of necessity back in 1999, when mobile carriers in Japan were struggling to support the messaging needs of eighty million users. Their hopes were that an emoji would reduce the need for multiple text messages or even picture messages.

1080. Based on statistics provided by the World Health Organization, there are around 360 million people in the world with disabling hearing loss, which represents nearly 5% of the entire world's population. Thirty two million of them are children between the ages of zero and fourteen.

1081. Dr. Duncan MacDougall from Haverhill once tried to demonstrate that the human soul had weight, so he placed dying patients on a giant scale. Amazingly, at the exact moment of death, there was a slight decrease in weight.

1082. In 2005, a man named Don Macpherson with a Ph.D. in glass science was playing ultimate Frisbee one day in Santa Cruz, California, when his friend asked him if he could wear sunglasses that he made himself. The friend immediately told him that he was no longer color blind.

1083. In the 1960's and 1970's, professional bowlers were seen as international celebrities. They even made twice as much money as NFL stars at the time.

1084. Over 300 species of spiders are known to mimic the outward appearance of ants, as a way to get close enough to eat them, or to avoid being eaten by them. It's a phenomenon called myrmecomorphy. These spiders have a false waist and are covered in reflective hair so that they can look shiny like the three-segmented bodies of ants. They also behave like ants by waving their front pairs of legs near their heads like antennae.

1085. The man who murdered John F. Kennedy Jr., Lee Harvey Oswald, was a US marine. He defected, however, and joined The Soviet Union in 1959, where he met his wife and had a child. In 1962, after deciding that he made a mistake moving to Russia, Oswald moved back to the US with his family.

1086. A whole genus of ferns was named after Lady Gaga. A DNA sequence spells out Gaga and the ferns have Gaga-like qualities. Some of them resemble her extravagant stage costumes and one of them is even called the Gaga Monstraparva.

1087. Alex's Lemonade Stand is a foundation started by Alexandra Scott after being diagnosed with neuroblastoma. In 2000, when she was four, she held a fundraiser with a lemonade stand in her front yard and raised $2,000. By the time of her death, in 2004, at the age of eight, she had raised more than one million dollars with the help of supporters from around the world.

1088. If Adidas finds any player having anything to do with Scientology, they will cancel any sponsorship deal they have.

1089. A man named Larry Walters attached forty five helium-filled weather balloons to a lawn chair and took off from San Pedro, Los Angeles, on July 2, 1992. He flew into controlled airspace near LAX airport and landed forty five minutes later on some power lines in Long Beach. Even though he was unhurt, he had to pay a $1,500 fine.

1090. In 1949, actor Ricardo Montalban was the first person to perform "Baby, it's Cold Outside," in the musical romantic comedy film "Neptune's Daughter." The actor is better known for playing the iconic villain Khan in the original Star Trek television series.

1091. The first woman to play for the Harlem Globetrotters was Lynette Woodard, in 1985. Since then, she has played in the WNBA and has been inducted into the Basketball Hall of Fame and Women's Basketball Hall of Fame.

1092. There is a housing complex in Montreal known as "Habitat

67" which is considered an architectural landmark and is also the most well known building in the city.

1093. Goosebumps serve an evolutionary purpose. They appear when the muscles beneath the body rise up to enable the hair to stand straight. The purpose is to get the whole outer coat to puff out to increase insulation and keep you warm.

1094. There are some species of scorpions that can live up to one year with no food or water.

1095. Before the Internet, hacking groups in the 1960's would take over phone lines using toys from cereal boxes. The whistles in Cap'n Crunch boxes could be played at 2,600 Hertz, creating a tone that could commandeer people's phone lines, allowing the hackers to make as many long distance phone calls as they wanted.

1096. According to the Dead Sea Scrolls and other various ancient manuscripts, Goliath stood at 6.75 inches (2.06 meters) tall. In contrast, the Masoretic Texts describe him to be 9.74 inches (2.97 meters) tall. Most scholars believe, however, that the shorter height was the accurate one.

1097. After the shooting of the 1970 film "The Private Life of Sherlock Holmes," starring Sir Christopher Lee, a movie prop of Nessie that sank to the bottom of Loch Ness was made.

1098. The "Hizamakura Lap Pillow" is a cushion pillow shaped like a woman's legs wearing a mini-skirt. It was created by Makoto Igarashib, in Tokyo, Japan, and you can lay your head down on it for maternal feelings.

1099. The first American woman to receive a patent was Mary Kies, from Connecticut, on May 15, 1809. Her innovation was to make a hat by weaving silk or thread into straw, creating a pleasing appearance that became a fashion fad.

1100. Author "Virginia Wade" has become renown by writing and publishing Bigfoot erotica novels on Amazon Kindle.

1101. In 1915, the city of San Diego experienced a severe drought. At one point, they hired a rain maker named Charles Hatfield, who referred to himself as a moisture accelerator, to solve the problem. He claimed to have concocted a chemical cocktail that would be released into the air and cause rainfall. Finally, on January 1, 1916, heavy rains started to fall on the city and prolonged for over a month, causing flood damage and almost fifty deaths. Eventually, the city declared the rain and floods were an act of God, so Hatfield was never paid for the job.

1102. There is a love motel for dogs in Sao Paulo, Brazil, with rooms decorated with satin sheets, romantic music, and heart-shaped ceiling mirrors. Renting a room for your dog for two hours costs about $50.

1103. In England, there is a statute that prohibits anyone from entering the Houses of Parliament wearing a suit of armor. This has been enforced since King Edward II decreed the law in 1313. It stated that "Every man shall come without force and armor."

1104. Bloom is a natural protective layer that coats eggs, sealing the pores to diminish moisture loss and preventing the development of bacteria.

1105. The Ministry of Environment, Energy, and the Sea in France is working on paving over 599 miles (965 kilometers) of road with solar panels. They expect that in around five years it will provide cheap and renewable energy to five million people.

1106. Having a dried llama fetus under the foundation of their homes is considered good luck for most Bolivian families. The animal fetus can usually be found at Bolivia's witch's market where you can also get toad talismans, owl feathers, and stone amulets.

1107. In 2005, a newborn baby was abandoned in a forest in Kenya. After two days, a stray dog found the baby and took him all the way back to her own litter of puppies.

1108. In 2016, Drake actually beat Michael Jackson's record for the most American Music Award nominations in one year. He had thirteen nominations, beating Jackson's record of eleven from 1984.

1109. Lobsters can regenerate lost eyes, claws, and antennae. You can also determine the gender of a lobster by looking at its swimmerets, the small feathery appendages on the underside of its tail. On males, the first pair of swimmerets closest to the body is hard and bony, while on females it's soft and feathery.

1110. Pablo Diego Jose Francisco de Paula Juan Nepomuceno Crispin Crispiniano María Remedios de la Santísima Trinidad Ruiz Picasso was actually Pablo Picasso's full name.

1111. Amish consider that formal school learning only provides limited value; that is why Amish kids only go to school until the eighth grade. They prefer to emphasize on agriculture as well as manual trades.

1112. YouTube has over one billion active users monthly. In comparison, Facebook has 1.8 billion, Instagram has 600 million, Twitter has 319 million, and Snapchat has an estimated 301 million.

1113. An Irish man named Alsan Dixon is known to master the art of the animal selfie. Although pictures look very casual, he sometimes spends hours gaining an animal's trust before a shot.

1114. In 2002, actor Steve Carell provided commentary track on the sports video game known as Outlaw Golf, while comedian Dave Attell did the commentary for Outlaw Golf 2.

1115. Australia has more wild camels that any other place in the world, including the Middle Eastern region. The high camel population has in fact become such a serious issue, that the government now spends tens of millions of dollars dealing with it.

1116. As of 2020, the highest grossing movie of all time is "Avengers: Endgame," surpassing Avatar from 2009. It brought in a little under $2.8 billion at the box office around the globe.

1117. According to the Down Syndrome Program at Boston Children's Hospital, a twenty five year old woman has a one in 1,200 chance of giving birth to a baby with Down Syndrome. The chances in a thirty five year-old mother are one in 350. The chances in a forty year old mother are one in 100. And a mother who's forty nine years old has a one in 10 chance.

1118. "LuDela" is a smart candle that can be lit and extinguished using a smartphone app.

1119. In the 1700's, coins were actually made of real gold and silver, so often criminals would shave down the sides of the coins and sell the shavings. Consequently, the US Mint began adding ridges to the coins, a process called reeding, to make it impossible to shave down without being detected, while also making counterfeiting more difficult. Today, no coins are made from precious metals, but the tradition has continued on coins of higher value. The reeding also helps the visually impaired to tell the difference between coins.

1120. A woman from Missouri named Edie Simms got herself arrested by the police so that she could cross "get arrested" off of her bucket list. The police officers were happy to handcuff her and take her to the police station so she could reach her goal.

1121. In May of 2007, a course on creating and maintaining a personal brand was actually co-taught by supermodel Tyra Banks at Stanford's Graduate School of Business.

1122. Methodes champenoise is a double fermentation process used to create champagne. The technique creates a lot of carbon dioxide that leads to an internal pressure of around five to six atmospheres, which is the equivalent of over eleven pounds (five kilograms) of weight on the glass. As a result, champagne bottles are much thicker and heavier, and their corks are held on by wire cages to prevent premature cork popping.

1123. According to Neil Degrasse Tyson, the galaxy called M87 is so gigantic that it contains around one trillion stars.

1124. Actor Tommy Lee Jones and Vice President Al Gore were freshmen roommates while at Harvard.

1125. According to a study led by Doctor Martin Nyffeler, the global population of spiders consumes 400 million to 800 million tons of insect prey per year. To put that into perspective, they consume nearly the same amount of prey as humans consume meat and fish yearly.

1126. The longest terrestrial mountain range is the Andes Mountains in South America, at 4,797 miles (7,725 kilometers) long. They cover a surface of more than 1,242,000 square miles (3,216,780 square kilometers), with an average mountain height of about 12,995 feet (3,962 meters).

1127. On average, the human small intestine is twenty feet long (six meters) and about one inch (2.54 centimeters) in diameter.

1128. The "London Booster" is a mechanical sculpture which was made by David Cerny to mark the 2012 London Summer Olympics. It's made from a double-decker bus from 1958, and it looks like an athlete with arms that mimic a pushup motion every day at three.

1129. The longest engagement on record lasted sixty seven years. Octavio Guillen and Adriana Martinez were both eighty-two years old when they finally got married in June of 1969, in Mexico City.

1130. In Saudi Arabia, the Starbucks logo only features a floating crown given that the original one, featuring a mermaid, is considered too vulgar to be displayed in this deeply religious and conservative country.

1131. The youngest king in British history to ascend to the British throne was Henry VI, the only child of King Henry V. He was only eight months and twenty five days old by then.

1132. In the Black Sea, there is a particular spot that preserves shipwrecks so well that scientists were able to see the builders' chisel marks in the wood. Forty one well-preserved ships were discovered there, which date back from the 9th century until the 19th century.

1133. Some cats actually love olives as they contain isoprenoids, which are structurally similar to the active chemical in catnip.

1134. Shigeki Tanaka watched Hiroshima get destroyed by the atomic bomb as he grew up in a neighboring town, and when he was twenty. Six years later he went to America, the country responsible for the bombing, participated in the Boston City marathon, and won the race on April 19, 1951.

1135. A study conducted at Washington University found that rats enjoy being tickled. High frequency recordings showed that they make the same laughing sound during a tickle session than when playing with other rats.

1136. The first robot-run hotel is named the Henn-na Hotel, meaning "strange hotel" in Japanese. Customers are greeted by multilingual robots at the front desk that help them check in or check out. At the coat room, a robotic arm stores your luggage for you and the porter robots carry them to your room.

1137. Elmo testified in front of the Congressional subcommittee on

Education Appropriations back in 2002, where he advocated for music research funding and more instruments for schools. He also went to the White House for an education event.

1138. A dog named Bobby walked over 2,485 miles (4,000 kilometers) across the US to reunite with his owners after he was separated from them on a family road trip.

1139. Approximately one liter of saliva is secreted by our mouths per day.

1140. Methyl anthranilate is the chemical used to flavor grape Kool Aid. Other uses of the chemical involve protecting crops such as corn, rice, and sunflowers as well as golf courses. It's also known to be used as a bird repellent.

1141. Brain maturity is not fully reached by most people until they are about twenty five years old. Until then they go through puberty.

1142. FIT is a footprint identification technique used by researchers to monitor cheetah populations in the wild. The technique considers every paw print unique to a particular cheetah, and it can be identified similarly to a human fingerprint.

1143. The annual Yukon Quest is regarded as the most difficult sled race worldwide, and it's held in February. It starts in Fairbanks in Alaska, and ends in White Horse, the Yukon Territory Capital (in Canada), which is 1,000 miles (1,609 kilometers) away. The event is really dangerous because of the extreme freezing weather, and the fact that participants can't seek assistance. Hans Gatt and his dogs set the record as the fastest team ever to complete the race, when in 2010, they finished the whole course in just nine days and twenty six minutes.

1144. The former CEO of the renowned virtual website "Neopets" was a Scientologist who used the org board method for his company. The method was actually designed by Scientology creator L. Ron Hubbard, making it the business model for his followers.

1145. Author Georges Perec wrote a 300-page French book called "A Void" without using the letter "E" even once. The book has since been translated into different languages, by scholars who also managed to avoid using the letter "E."

1146. People with bumper stickers are more likely to have road rage and be involved in accidents according to research conducted at Colorado State University.

1147. One of the world's first private pilots was magician and escape artist Harry Houdini. During his maiden flight in Germany, he actually crashed, but he continued practicing and eventually set his sights on becoming the first man to pilot an airplane in Austria.

1148. The water used to baptize all royal babies is brought from the river Jordan, as it is where it is said that Jesus was baptized by John the Baptist.

1149. Between 2006 and 2012, fishing was the activity that accounted for the most lightning strikes and deaths, with a total of twenty six deaths.

1150. China has a law that makes it illegal not to visit your parents regularly if they are over sixty.

1151. Dr. Ruth, the famous author, American sex therapist, and media personality, was actually trained as a sniper when she was just sixteen years old by the Jewish military organization Haganah, in Israel.

1152. Riding a roller coaster is one of the most effective ways to dislodge a kidney stone, according to a 2018 Michigan State University study. Of all roller coasters tested, it was found that Disneyland's Big Thunder Mountain was the most effective of all.

1153. In Alaska, there was a serial killer man named Robert Hansen. He used to kidnap young women and take them to his cabin. Later, he would release them into the woods and hunt them down with a rifle and knife. Hansen was convicted in 1984 and died in 2014.

1154. The lightest metal ever made is called microlattice. It's so light that it can literally rest on the top of a dandelion. Although it's about 99.99% air, it's made entirely from metal, and 100 times lighter than styrofoam.

1155. After his death in 1506, Christopher Columbus actually kept on traveling. After he died, he was buried in Valladolid, Spain. However, three years later, his remains were taken to his family in a mausoleum in Sevilla. In 1542, his remains were moved to Santo Domingo, Hispañola, in accordance with his son's will. Then, in 1795, his bones were moved to Havana. Finally, more than a hundred years later, his remains were sent back to Sevilla in 1898.

1156. Since the year 1280, at least four powerful earthquakes have hit the region where the Leaning Tower of Pisa is. In fact, the tower has survived because of the soft soil underneath it.

1157. The role of James Bond was offered to Liam Neeson who was up for the role, but had to turn it down as his girlfriend at the time said she wouldn't marry him if he took it.

1158. A gun that could shoot darts causing heart attacks was once created by the CIA and revealed during a congressional testimony in 1975. The dart only left a tiny red dot upon penetration of the skin, but the poison itself worked rapidly and then denatured quickly afterwards.

1159. Ralph Lauren, the iconic designer, was named Ralph Lifshitz until he was sixteen. He and his brother Jerry were made fun of in school, so they both changed their surname to Lauren.

1160. The procedure of transferring stool from a healthy donor into a gastrointestinal tract of a patient is called fecal transplant. The procedure is done when antibiotics kill off too many of the good bacteria in the digestive system.

1161. The first primetime TV show to have a sound of a flushing toilet was "All in the Family." Before, it was actually taboo to even show a bathroom on TV.

1162. Originally, the traffic and train light for go was white while caution was green. However, the white light for go caused several accidents. In 1914 for example, one of the red lenses fell out of its holder leaving a white light behind; this ended up with a train running a stop signal and crashing into another train. As a result, the railroad changed it so that the green light means go and yellow was chosen for caution, mainly because it's the most distinct color from the other two.

1163. The national animal of Indonesia is the Komodo dragon.

1164. The largest bonfire ever was held in Norway, on June 27, 2016, which measured 155 feet (forty seven meters) in the air.

1165. In 1996, the commencement address to 245 graduates at Southampton College was delivered by Kermit the Frog.

1166. Lots of different animal species experience the Coolidge effect. The effect is named after US President Calvin Coolidge, and it refers to a biological anomaly, where males show renewed sexual interest when a new female is added to a group.

1167. According to the Center for Disease Control, people with weak immune systems are more at risk for contracting bacteria.

1168. To be born, the babies of a female sea louse actually chew their way out of the mother's insides.

1169. The Warner Brothers started creating short animations to promote the music they owned in the early 1930's. They're known as "Looney Tunes."

1170. You can find over 582,000 Buddhas in the Thanboddhay Pagoda Temple in Myanmar.

1171. Justin Bieber's single "Baby" is the most disliked music video on the Internet. It has over 9.9 million dislikes on YouTube and over two billion views.

1172. The only two animals in the world who engage in tongue kissing are humans and bonobo chimpanzees.

1173. Since 2005, thirty six years old Michael Jackson's pet chimpanzee Bubbles has been living at The Center for Great Apes sanctuary in Wauchula, Florida. When Bubbles lived with Michael Jackson, the young chimp slept in a crib and ate candy at Neverland Ranch. However, when it became fully mature and aggressive, he was taken away by an animal trainer to ensure the safety of Jackson.

1174. In 2017, Tostitos, Uber, and Mothers Against Drunk Driving, worked together to design an alcohol detecting chip bag for the Superbowl. The top of the bag had a sensor that could analyze a person's breath. If you had been drinking, a red steering wheel would appear on the bag along with a "Don't drink and drive" warning. If you were sober, green flashing lights would appear underneath the logo on the bag.

1175. According to scientists, Ramses II, the ancient Egyptian Pharaoh, lived to be either ninety two or ninety six years old, outliving many of his older sons. Through CT scans, scientists also found that Ramses II had red hair, as well as arthritis in his hip, and gum disease.

1176. The "Wreck of the Titan" was a novella written by author Morgan Robertson in 1898. In the book the ship Titan sinks in the north Atlantic after being hit by an iceberg. The story of the sinking is strangely similar to the actual Titanic, which sank just fourteen years after the book was released. Both ships were deemed to be unsinkable, didn't have enough lifeboats, struck an iceberg, and sank and lost more than half of their passengers.

1177. The fear of baldness is called peladophobia.

1178. If you clamp your nostrils and mouth shut during a sneeze, your eardrums or sinuses could be damaged or it can cause an ear infection. Sneezes are actually quite powerful; the sudden expulsion of air can propel mucus droplets at rates of up to one hundred miles (160 kilometers) per hour.

1179. In the Philippines, Balut is considered a national delicacy. It consists of a fertilized duck egg or duck embryo that is boiled and then eaten from the shell.

1180. The "water phone" is an instrument that makes many of the scary sounds that you hear in thriller and horror movies.

1181. In 1991, a man named Steve Feltam gave up everything he had to look for the Loch Ness Monster full time. He quit his job, sold his house, left his girlfriend, bought a 1970 camper van, and has been living in it by Lake Loch Ness ever since. He also holds the current Guinness World Record for the longest time spent looking for the Loch Ness Monster.

1182. Your organs and tissues aren't the only ones made of water. Your skeletal system contains water, and 31% of your bone mass is water.

1183. According to scientists, studying the earwax of a blue whale can reveal important aspects of its life. The technique is described in the proceedings of the National Academy of Sciences and it's considered a tool to understand the whale's hormonal and chemical biography. It can also provide information about how long discontinued pollutants can still pervade and affect the environment today.

1184. Viggo Mortensen, who starred in "Lord of the Rings," actually bought the two horses he rode when making the movies. He also bought the one he rode at the set of Hidalgo.

1185. There is an animal called the pronghorn antelope which has vision ten times better than the average human. Scientists believe that this animal can see the rings of Saturn on a clear night.

1186. Bees can see ultraviolet wavelengths. In fact, they are attracted to flowers because petals have UV patterns on them.

1187. In Boyne Valley, Ireland, there's an ancient temple that predates the Great Pyramids of Giza and the Stonehenge. It's known as "Newgrange," and it was constructed by farmers from the Stone Age, about 5,200 years ago. It's a circular grass thatched mound that's 278 feet (eighty five meters) in diameter, and forty four feet (thirteen meters) high.

1188. The "Ruggie" is an alarm clock device disguised as a rug. It has a sensor that will only turn off the alarm once you have stepped on it for at least three seconds, forcing you to get out of bed. It also has speakers that will deliver motivational quotes that you can choose to start your day right.

1189. Located in Tokyo, Butler Café is staffed by waiters who are all butlers. You can ask them to address you as "Princess" or "Prince," and they'll comply.

1190. It was actually perfectly legal to possess and consume alcohol privately during America's Prohibition Era. Only the production, importation, transportation and sale of alcohol was outlawed.

1191. After the assassination of Abraham Lincoln, his body was taken on a two-week, 1,600-mile (2,574 kilometer) tour by train. Also the body of his son, William Wallace Lincoln, who had died of typhoid fever at the age of eleven, and buried in the DC area in 1862, was taken along with it. The tour involved 400 train stations and viewings were arranged where his body was on display for mourners.

1192. The only man to be struck by lightning seven times according to Guinness World Records was the ex-park ranger Roy C. Sullivan. He suffered a lost toenail, lost eyebrows, a shoulder injury, leg burns, an ankle injury, chest and stomach burns, and had his hair set on fire twice.

1193. The Anelosimus Eximius is a breed of social spider that works with others, building some of the largest spider webs in the world. Over 50,000 spiders can live on one web until they eventually outgrow it and have to form new colonies.

1194. There were so many lobsters when the first European settlers reached North America that they washed ashore in piles up to twenty four inches (sixty one centimeters high).

1195. Originally, the chainsaw was developed to assist with giving birth by Cesarean section and not for cutting wood.

1196. Felix Batista was a hostage negotiator, who, in 2008, was kidnapped in Mexico after presenting on how to survive when kidnapped. He has not been found to this day.

1197. During the cold winters, the Alaskan wood frog shapes itself as a block of ice. It literally stops breathing and its heart stops beating. When spring arrives, the frog then thaws and returns to normal life.

1198. Sweetwater, in Texas, holds a three day rattlesnake round-up every single spring. Snake hunters bring in their catches, which end up being thousands of snakes, for which they are paid five dollars for every pound (0.45 kilograms). The tradition began back in 1958 by the Junior Chamber of Commerce as a way to address the overpopulation of snakes.

1199. A study done by the University of Vienna found that the older a father is when he has a child the less attractive the child will be.

1200. There is a vending machine in Istanbul that gives water and food to dogs in exchange for recyclable bottles.

1201. The artist who has performed the most concerts in Madison Square Garden than any other singer is Billy Joel.

1202. On June 17, 1955, a land mine that was planted during World War I, in 1917, was struck by lightning and killed a cow. The rare event made the cow a casualty of war thirty eight years later.

1203. The tarantula hawk wasp is said to have one of the most painful stings of all known insects. The pain subsides after three minutes, but experts suggest that if it ever stings you, you'd better just lie on the ground, and start screaming. Few people if any are able to maintain their coordination after getting stung, so chances are you'll end up hurting yourself worse as you desperately look for a way to ease your agony.

1204. In 2017, RAND conducted a study that showed that 60% of American adults suffer at least from one chronic condition, and 42% suffer from more than one. This actually represents hundreds of billions of dollars spent on healthcare every year.

1205. The Kleine-Levin syndrome or Sleeping Beauty syndrome is a very unusual disorder where those affected sleep for up to twenty hours per day for days, weeks, or even months at a time; they only wake to use the restroom or to eat.

1206. Belgian national Stefaan Engels, at age forty nine, ran a record setting marathon in 2010 for 365 consecutive days. He started in Belgium and finished in Barcelona, running 9,321 miles (15,000 kilometers), and crossing seven countries along the way.

1207. There is not a single land snake in New Zealand. They do have sea snakes however.

1208. Elon Musk didn't like the school that his kids were going to so he made his own called "Ad Astr" which means "to the stars."

1209. The holiday favorite, mistletoe, is actually a parasite that lives by sucking the nutrients from trees. When it spreads to the branches, the tree dies. Despite this, the parasite feeds birds, may treat cancer, and inspires kissing.

1210. There is only one stop sign in all of Paris.

1211. There is a large Roman Catholic church in Barcelona named the Sagrada Famila that began construction in 1882 and won't be completed until 2026.

1212. India and Colombia are the two countries with the most public holidays. Per year, they both have eighteen holidays.

1213. "Froggyland" is a museum in Croatia that exhibits 507 stuffed frogs. The frogs are actually the work of 20th century Hungarian taxidermist Ferenc Mere, who spent ten years stuffing and meticulously organizing the frogs.

1214. Victor Lustig, a maverick con man, sold the Eiffel Tower for scrap in 1925 to a metal buyer who gave him a large bribe in cash, thinking that he was a corrupt French Government official. The buyer discovered he was scammed when he went to claim the Paris landmark, but by then, Lustig had run away to Austria.

1215. Before the Grand Prix featured sponsor decorated vehicles, the cars had the colors of the countries they were from. Germany's team used to have a white car, but in 1934, it came in overweight, so they peeled off all the lead paint, leaving a silver shining car. As a result, Germany changed its color to silver, and Mercedes Benz was inspired to make the famous race cars.

1216. Every August 31 since 1922, El Salvador has held an annual tradition called "Los Bolos del Juego," or balls of fire, where two groups of young people throw flaming balls of old cloth and wire that are soaked in gas at each other.

1217. Washing your hands with soap is more effective to kill bacteria and prevent disease than any vaccine out there according to the World Health Organization.

1218. The last woman over forty years old to have a number one song and Billboard Hot 100 chart as a lead artist is singer Sia, with the song "Cheap Thrills." Before her, the last woman to do so was Bette Midler, in 1989, with the song "Wind beneath My Wings," when she was forty three years old.

1219. In Aberdeen, Washington, which is Kurt Cobain's hometown, there is a sign welcoming visitors that says "Come As You Are," after Nirvana's hit song.

1220. Based on several descriptions, the Colossus of Rhodes, the ancient Greek statue, was about the same height as the Statue of Liberty in New York City.

1221. A total distance of 1.74 billion miles (2.7 billion kilometers) has to be traveled by NASA's robotic spacecraft Juno to arrive on the planet Jupiter. It launched from Cape Canaveral on August 5, 2011, and arrived on Jupiter on July 4, 2016.

1222. In 2010, a biker gang in Denmark called "Black Cobra" once took 120 boxes of almond tarts, punsch rolls, apple crowns, and brownies from a delivery truck.

1223. In Liechtenstein, the incarceration rate is nineteen people for every one hundred thousand. The country's population is only thirty seven thousand meaning they only have seven people in their jail.

1224. Because of the extremely high ductility of gold, a single ounce of gold, which is twenty eight grams, can be stretched into a wire that is about fifty six miles (ninety kilometers) long.

1225. The tongues of woodpeckers are made up of bone and cartilage. They use them to wrap around their skulls in order to protect their heads. Whenever they peck wood, their tongues absorb the shock that's given to the brain and skull.

1226. The Moulage Museum in Zurich, Switzerland, is a museum dedicated to wax representations of disfiguring diseases. In the past, civilizations as old as the ancient Egyptians used wax to record how people looked when they died.

1227. American Presidents who've served from January 1, 1997, onwards are to be given life-long secret service protection along with their spouses, according to a law passed in December, 2012. The protection extends to any of their children aged sixteen or under.

1228. According to a memo from a top franchisee, only one out of every five millennials has ever tried a Big Mac.

1229. Certain studies carried out by the Indiana University Media School showed that watching cat videos seems to boost viewers' energy and positive emotions.

1230. Rabbits are able to sleep with their eyes open. They go into a trance-like state, which makes them only half asleep. The advantage of this is that, in the wild, it allows them to be more alert and get away from predators in a hurry.

1231. In many different instances, nuclear reactors in various countries have been powered down because of overheating. Strangely, jellyfish has been the cause of the problems in these cases. The creature clogs up water intakes in the reactor cooling systems, and it has to be taken out before the reactor can work properly again.

1232. "The Spirit of Ecstasy" is actually what the hood ornament on a Rolls Royce car is called.

1233. Garfield's illustrator Jim Davis almost chooses pizza over lasagna as the character's favorite food, as it was easier to draw, but he ultimately changed his mind. The lovable and lazy cat's favorite dish first appeared in the comic strip on July 15, 1978, where he says: "It's nature's most perfect food."

1234. Researchers at the University of Helsinki have found that running in shoes that are highly cushioned make your legs stiffer and increase impact loading. Research proved that extra cushioned shoes actually alter the spring-like mechanisms of running.

1235. Some Maltese churches have two clocks. The one placed on the right side reads the correct time, and is used by the faithful to know when to go to mass. The one on the left is set to read the wrong time, supposedly to confuse the devil so he can't disrupt the church services.

1236. "Marmot Day" is Alaska's own version of Groundhog Day, as there are no groundhogs in the region.

1237. The popular saying "bless you" after a sneeze originated from the 14th century, when Pope Gregory the VII asked for it to be said after every time he sneezed so he could be protected against the plague.

1238. Due to genetics, if your parents or grandparents have a history of multiple cavities or dentures at an early age, you have a higher risk from suffering the same outcome.

1239. Math Pics is an iOS app that can answer math equations in seconds. The way it works is that you take a picture of a hand-written math problem and it will give you the answer as well as step by step directions on how it got there.

1240. The news about the assassination of President Abraham Lincoln reached London eleven days after the fatal event happened.

1241. On June 24 every year, people in the Philippines hold the Roasted Pig Parade to celebrate the feast of Saint John the Baptist. They roast pigs and then dress them up with sunglasses, bridal attire, or even wigs.

1242. "The Boring Conference" is an annual conference where people in the past have given talks on barcodes, sneezing, and the sounds of vending machines, among other boring topics.

1243. Back in the 1800's, the teeth from dead soldiers were removed and used to make dentures for the rich whose teeth were rotten.

1244. There is a school located in Atule'er village, in southwest China, where some students between the ages of six and fifteen have to climb a cliff about 2,624 feet (800 meters) high in order to get to the school, taking about ninety minutes to do so.

1245. On February 10, 2017, there was a full moon, a lunar eclipse, and a comet that passed by. All three of them could be seen in the same night.

1246. The 1942 musical film "Holiday Inn," starring Bing Crosby, gave the name to the popular Holiday Inn Hotel chain.

1247. In the United States, the average dental student graduates with over $261,000 of debt. That is actually four times more from what it used to be in 1990.

1248. In the mountains of the Canary Islands, there is a language that consists of whistling and has been used for centuries. It's called Silbo Gomero and it's used by transferring Spanish into whistling sounds, which makes the messages travel further and louder than if you were to yell.

1249. In the Czech Republic, the representation of Santa Claus or Father Christmas doesn't exist. However, children there believe that Baby Jesus brings them Christmas gifts.

1250. Urea, the main ingredient in urine, actually has properties to unboil an eggwhite in just a matter of a few minutes.

1251. A small LED light bulb can actually be powered by the electricity that is made from the human brain.

1252. A passenger flight from Moscow to Hong Kong called Aeroflot flight 593 crashed into a mountain range killing everyone on board. Eventually it was known that the pilot let his children temporarily fly the plane, but his sixteen year old son unintentionally deactivated the autopilot controls. The pilots ended up over correcting and crashed the plane.

1253. In 2016, thirty two year old Joey Jaws Chestnut from California reclaimed his title by winning the Annual Nathan's Hot Dog Eating Contest, held at Coney Island. He had seventy hot dogs in just ten minutes, which is one hot dog every 8.6 seconds.

1254. The US is the only country worldwide that prints all its currency in the same size and color. Consequently, 3.3 million blind and visually-impaired Americans depend on someone else to identify the denomination of each bill.

1255. Famous soccer player Cristiano Ronaldo has the most Instagram followers with over 214 million followers.

1256. Will Smith got so attached to the German Shepherd in "I am Legend" that he asked if he could buy her, but the dog owner refused.

1257. "Pick a Melon" is an app that helps you pick a ripe watermelon. The way it works is that you place the microphone of your smartphone on the watermelon, knock on the melon until all three test lights are glowing, and wait for the result.

1258. In 1971, women in Switzerland were conceded the right to vote. From all the way back to 1291, the men of Switzerland exercised their democratic right to deny voting rights to their mothers, daughters and sisters.

1259. In Japan, a team of biologists at The Osaka University discovered a new way to grow parts of the human eye (the retina, cornea, lens, etc.) simply by using a small sample of adult skin.

1260. Up until the late 1960's, Disneyland used to ban long-haired male visitors to their park with the excuse that they didn't meet the unwritten dress code.

1261. Forty eight hours after quitting smoking, your sense of smell and taste begin to improve dramatically.

1262. The province of Newfoundland was once an independent dominion that functioned much like its own country until 1934. On March 31, 1949, it became a part of Canada, after a referendum where 52% of voters supported joining the country.

1263. Famous artist Leonardo da Vinci was born out of wedlock, that's why he never had a last name. The "da Vinci" part of his name actually comes from the town Vinci where he was born, so his name means Leonardo of Vinci.

1264. There is a bank in Italy known as the Credem Bank that accepts cheese from local producers in exchange for cheap loans. The bank currently holds over four hundred thousand wheels of Parmesan cheese which is worth almost two hundred million Euros.

1265. In 2014, in the Cappadocia region of Turkey, a massive underground city was discovered. It had everything from churches, waterways, fountains, kitchens, and even wineries and oil presses. The city is the size of sixty-five football fields and housed about 20,000 people at the time.

1266. Jerry Springer, talk show host and the king of racy TV, used to be in politics. As a matter of fact, he was the Mayor of Cincinnati for an entire year, from 1977 to 1978.

1267. The human scalp has on average 100,000 hair follicles.

1268. Chicken Run is the highest grossing stop motion animation film starring Mel Gibson. It was filmed in the year 2000.

1269. In Paris, a law was approved that allows anyone to plant an urban garden anywhere within the city.

1270. Until the 1970's, the bluefin tuna was considered a trash fish and it was used to make cat food or hauled off to the dumps. It had such a bad reputation in Japan that they called it "nekomatagi," which translates to food too low for even a cat to eat.

1271. Frankenstein's monster was never actually given a name, but he tells his creator, Victor Frankenstein, that he should be called Adam (based on Adam in the Bible). Victor, however, does not refer to the monster as Adam, but he uses instead various insulting names like devil, the demon, specter, thing, being, and ogre.

1272. At one point in time, lemurs in Madagascar were so big that they were the size of today's male gorillas.

1273. In Shanghai, if you don't send greetings or visit your elderly parents, your credit score can get lowered.

1274. The ex-wife of singer Freddie Mercury, Mary Austin, is the only person who knows where the singer's ashes are laid to rest as she buried them herself. She has said that she will never reveal where they are buried.

1275. Near Newark, in Ohio, there's a building shaped like a picnic basket. It was built in 1997 by Dave Longaberger, owner of Longaberger Basket Company, to be used as his head office.

1276. On July 1, 1941, the first ever TV commercial was shown in the United States. It was a shaky ten-second commercial for Bulova Watches, which was aired just before a Brooklyn Dodgers and Philadelphia Phillies baseball game.

1277. There are 3D printers that can print food. The "Foodini Food Printer" can print anything from pizza to burgers to chocolate, using fresh ingredients.

1278. It's possible for crocodiles to hold their breath underwater for up to two hours. The colder the water, the longer that they can stay under, given that crocodiles use more energy and oxygen in warm water.

1279. By just spinning an egg you can tell the difference of a hard-cooked one from a raw one. If it spins easily, it's hard-cooked. If it wobbles, it's raw.

1280. March 1 was designated as the New Year in the early Roman calendar. It had ten months, which is still reflected in some of the names of the months. For example, September through to December, our ninth through to twelfth months, were originally positioned as the seventh through tenth months. Septum is Latin for seven, Octo is eight, Novem is nine, and Decem is ten.

1281. President James A. Garfield was assassinated less than four months after becoming president. The shot he received in the back was not fatal as it did not hit any of his vital organs, and the bullet lodged behind his pancreas. Later, it was found that it was the doctors who actually killed him.

1282. In Icelandic folklore, the Yule Cat is a vicious creature that hunts and eats people who did not receive any garments or clothes to wear for Christmas.

1283. The 8998 butterfly is a subspecies of butterfly. Its name comes from its wing markings, which uncannily resemble the number eighty nine on one wing, and the number ninety eight on the other.

1284. The best time to spray perfume onto yourself is right after a bath or shower. The scent lasts longer when it's applied to hydrated skin.

1285. About 20,000 bees followed and swarmed a sixty eight year old grandmother's car for two days in West Wales. The bees were actually trying to rescue their queen bee, which unbeknownst to her, had hitched a ride in her Mitsubishi Outlander. Beekeepers were brought in to safely remove them.

1286. Alfred Binet invented the IQ test as a method to identify students who needed help. He actually disapproved the use of the test as a ranking for unitary and linear intelligence.

1287. At the back of their nose, dogs have a secondary organ for smelling. It's called the Jacobson's organ, and it boosts the canines' sense of smell so much that dogs have the ability to smell cancer on patients' breaths.

1288. Research conducted by scientists from Psychology Today concluded that if a person's body odor smells good to you, it means that their immunity genes are opposite to yours. This allows higher chances for people with opposite immunity genes to mate, which results in descendants with stronger immune systems.

1289. Many astronauts after returning home from trips to space report letting go of objects in midair, still expecting them to float.

1290. There are approximately 40,000 unclaimed bodies in morgues across the United States according to sixwise.com. Some of them have no family or the family members aren't able to afford the cost of burials or cremation.

1291. As a way to thank actor Harrison Ford who narrated a documentary for the London Museum of Natural History in 1994, a spider species discovered in 1993 was named Calponia Harrisonfordi. The spider is very tiny, it measures around 0.19 inches (five millimeters) in length, and lives in California.

1292. The volcanic explosion of Mount St. Helens on May 18, 1980, remains as the fastest recorded avalanche in history, reaching a speed of 250 miles (400 kilometers) per hour.

1293. In the Sacred Valley, in Peru, there is an accommodation facility called "The Skylodge Adventure Suites" that offers a unique chance to sleep in a completely transparent hanging bedroom capsule over 1,000 feet (305 meters) above the valley floor. The capsules measure 23.9 feet (7.3 meters) in length and

7.8 feet (2.4 meters) in height and width; it has four beds, a dining area, and a bathroom.

1294. It has been proved that people who play action games are better learners. As they excel at predicting the sequence of upcoming events, they become better learners by playing fast-paced games.

1295. In order to make the World War II movie "Fury" more realistic, actor Shia LeBeouf cut his own face and had his dentist pull out one of his teeth.

1296. The psychological act of repeating a word or phrase over and over again until it loses its meaning to the listener is called "semantic satiation."

1297. It was found that 70% of US athletes have a rare gene variant in their heart, known as ACTN3, making them great sprinters. In fact, 75% of all Jamaicans have this gene.

1298. In Japan, the workers of Maruyama Zoo were attempting to get two hyenas to mate for four years until they realised they were both males.

1299. A study done by the University of Chicago discovered that people think more rationally and make better choices in their second language.

1300. All members of the Wu-Tang Clan are in the top twenty artists with the biggest vocabularies in the world.

1301. Coconuts can be classified as fruits, nuts, or seeds. Many people consider them to be the tree of life as every part of a coconut can be used as food, fiber, drink, utensils, fuel, and even instruments.

1302. Israeli company Tactical Robots built a drone ambulance called the AirMule that can take off and land vertically. It was designed for conditions where landing a helicopter is not viable, for example on a battlefield. It can carry up to 991 pounds (450 kilograms) for up to thirty one miles (fifty kilometers).

1303. Billionaire David Tepper once paid $43.5 million for a beachfront mansion just to later demolish it. The previous owner of the mansion was actually Tepper's former boss, who denied him a promotion when both worked together.

1304. On September 9, 1999, at 9:09 AM, Nicholas Steven Waddle was born, also weighing in at nine pounds nine ounces (around four kilograms).

1305. The Apollo 11 moon landing took less computing power than a Google search query takes today.

1306. It's well documented that ducks sometimes float through tidal rapids in fast flowing river stretches, and upon getting to the end, rush back upstream to do it over again.

1307. In 1864, during the US Civil War, the Battle of Cherbourg took place. It involved a single ship battle between the Union warship USS Kearsarge and the Confederate warship CSS Alabama. The battle happened off the coast of France, in the English Channel. The CSS Alabama eventually lost and sank.

1308. There are no felon voting restrictions in the states of Maine and Vermont. This means that even current inmates can vote.

1309. The only quadripoint on Earth where four different countries meet is in Africa among the countries of Namibia, Botswana, Zimbabwe, and Zambia.

1310. In the 2015 Disney film "Moana," retired NFL safety, Troy Polamalu had a minor speaking role.

1311. Out of all the natural lakes in the world, over half of them can be found in Canada.

1312. When Wolfgang Amadeus Mozart was only seven years old, he proposed marriage to Marie Antoinette, who was also the same age.

1313. Tigers' night vision is six times better than humans. They have a retinal adaptation that reflects light back to the retina, making their night vision more powerful.

1314. Between 1934 and 1938, while gangster Al Capone was imprisoned in Alcatraz for tax evasion, he was permitted to play the banjo in the prison band that he helped form due to his good behavior. The band was named Rock Islanders and they performed every Sunday for the other inmates.

1315. The most polluted river in the world is the Citarum River located in Indonesia which contains dyes, chemicals and various other substances.

1316. The second non US born First Lady is Melania Trump. The first one was Louisa Catherine Adams, wife of John Adams, the sixth President of the United States.

1317. Oysters change their sex from male to female and back several times during their lifetime.

1318. Giant catfish in parts of Europe have been known to deliberately beach themselves so as to quickly attack birds such as pigeons. After catching the bird, they flop back into the water and drown the bird, just like alligators do.

1319. Some studies suggest that gifted people tend to have bad handwriting because their brains are normally working faster than their hand.

1320. Kyu-Shirataki is the name of a defunct train station located on the island of Hokkaido, Japan. The station operates just for one girl, so that she can attend school every day. The train only makes two trips: one when the high school student leaves for school and the other when she returns.

1321. The grasshopper mouse defends its territory by standing up on its back legs, and producing a high-pitched howling sound in the same manner as a wolf.

1322. Inspired by KFC fried chicken scented sunscreen, Edmonton's La Poutine Restaurant and Food Truck collaborated with the Wild Prairie Soap Company to create a poutine-flavored lip balm, which has been sold out almost everywhere since its release.

1323. When Bill Gates was worth over thirty billion dollars in 1997, he was still seen catching economy class in the air.

1324. According to historian Andrew Mahain Sutherland, there was a mountain man in the 1800's named John Johnson who went by the nickname "Liver-Eating Johnson" because he ate the livers of about 300 Crow Indians. The reason he did this was to revenge the murder of his wife, who was from the Flathead American Indian tribe. The consumption of their livers was considered an insult to the Crow because they believe that they were important for the afterlife. After making peace with the tribe eventually, John died at the age of seventy five in Santa Monica, California in 1900.

1325. In the United States, if you are missing a toe, you will not be allowed into the armed forces. To join, it's mandatory that you have both feet totally intact, despite the fact it's possible to run even without your big toe.

1326. Masked birch caterpillars use anal drumming to call other young caterpillars to help spin silk for their cocoons and maintain them. To cause the vibrations, they rub hairs on their rear ends against a leaf.

1327. The most recent test of a nuclear bomb goes to North Korea, according to the Guinness World Record, which happened on May 25, 2009.

1328. At the moment, there are about 1,400 asteroids in space that have the potential for creating a hazard, and they would result in serious devastation if they collided with Earth.

1329. During World War II, a band on the USS Arizona called the USS Arizona Band were all killed during the bombing of Pearl Harbor.

1330. The shark prop used in the 1975 movie "Jaws" was named "Bruce" by Steven Spielberg after his lawyer.

1331. According to a study published in the Journal of Neurobiology of Aging, the more flights of stairs a person climbs or the more years of school a person completes, the younger the brain physically looks. Jason Steffener, a scientist and researcher at Concordia's Center, found that the brain age decreases by 0.95 years for each year of education, and it decreases 0.58 years for every daily flight of stairs climbed.

1332. Back in 2007, late night talk show host Conan O'Brien was being stalked by a priest, who was later arrested. The priest was writing threatening notes on parish letterheads, contacting his parents, and showing up at his studio. He even referred to himself as "your priest stalker."

1333. Durian is a type of fruit from Asia that smells so bad that Singapore banned it on their Rapid Mass Transit systems. The odor is described as turpentine and onions garnished with a gym sock, according to food writer Richard Sterling.

1334. During the 18th century, British wealthy landowners would hire hermits to live on their land for aesthetic purposes. These hermits would only live on their estate and think about their existence while providing wisdom with visitors. One ad that was looking for a hermit, however, demanded that they could not talk to anyone, cut their hair, or even leave the estate.

1335. One of the highest literacy rates in the whole world is found in Cuba, at 99.8%.

1336. In 2027, the autopsy report for Elvis Presley is expected to be unsealed for the first time, which will be fifty years after his death.

1337. "Frog" is the term given to the underside of a horse's hoof.

1338. Researchers at the National University of Singapore discovered that the Chinese soft shell turtle is able to pee out of its mouth. They noticed that turtles would stick their heads into puddles of water and wiggle their tongues, but they weren't drinking.

1339. Women in the Victorian era would wear hats decorated with dead birds treated with arsenic. Today, some of these hats are on display in museums and still have traces of arsenic on them.

1340. Queen Elizabeth conferred Bill Gates with an honorary knighthood, but because he's American, he cannot use the title Sir.

1341. A liger is the result of mixing a white lion and a tiger. The world's first ligers were born in 2013, a white lion and a tiger had four male cubs which are now the rarest big cats on Earth.

1342. The first American president to be given a secret service code name was former president Harry S. Truman, who served from 1945 to 1953. His code name was General.

1343. Most mammals have the same number of vertebrae in their necks, which are seven. The only two that do not have exactly seven vertebrae are sloths and manatees.

1344. Tesla doesn't have a marketing budget and instead puts all its money into making their product as good as possible.

1345. The oldest person to ever visit the South Pole was famous astronaut and adventurer Buzz Aldrin, in 2016, at the age of eighty six. However, after he began to experience altitude sickness and was short of breath, he had to evacuate.

1346. Director and daughter of Francis Ford Coppola, Sofia Coppola, actually appeared in all three of her father's Godfather movies.

1347. The acronym SHAZAM shouted to conjure up comic book hero Captain Marvel stands for Solomon, Hercules, Atlas, Zeus, Achilles, and Mercury.

1348. There is a group of blind millipedes that glow in the dark, giving off a neon teal color, in California's Sierra Nevada Mountains. The millipedes have a special type of protein that allows them to produce light from beneath the tough cuticle that covers their bodies.

1349. Famous actor Joe Pesci from hit movies such as "GoodFellas" and "My Cousin Vinny" released a rap song called "Wise Guy" in 1998. He said that originally he wanted to be a musician, but his father pushed him into acting.

1350. After a successful career as a heavyweight champion, George Foreman became the pastor of North Houston's "Church of the Lord Jesus Christ." The sixty eight year old reverend was inspired to join the church as he himself grew up in poverty and wanted to help others.

1351. Nagasaki was destroyed by a nuclear bomb, and just a few weeks later, members of the team that dropped the bomb toured the devastated city. They all kept their real identities secret for the trip, but they managed to talk to some Japanese locals.

1352. There is a six thousand year old baobab tree in South Africa that is so big that it could fit a small building inside of it.

1353. When playing Monopoly with his kids, Pablo Escobar used to cheat, hiding extra money ahead of time near where he planned to sit.

1354. People's obsession with bacon over the past decade has led to some really strange bacon products, such as bacon ice cream, bacon lollipops, bacon mayonnaise, bacon chocolate bars, and bacon gumballs.

1355. In 1948, a local man named Tony Signorini would put on a pair of 29.9 pound (13.6 kilogram), three-toed shoes and walk along the beaches in Florida at night, creating huge footprints in the sand. Locals believed that a 14.7 foot (4.5 meter) tall penguin was roaming the beaches until the mystery was solved in 1988.

1356. About 554 million tacos from the fast food chain "Jack in the Box" are eaten every year according to the Wall Street Journal.

1357. In the Orion constellation's sword portion, the middle star isn't an actual start. That's the Orion Nebula, and it's the only nebula that can be seen with naked eyes from our planet.

1358. In 1925, a huge Sequoia tree found in California's Kings Canyon National Park was named the country's national Christmas tree. It measured 298.4 feet (ninety one meters).

1359. The horse head used when filming "The Godfather" was actually a real one. Actor John Marley was not informed beforehand, so his scream was authentic, not scripted at all.

1360. Birds in cities often use cigarette butts for their nests as the nicotine inside them repels parasites.

1361. There is a book named "Becoming Batman - The Possibility of a Superhero." It was published by a neuroscience professor in 2008 exploring the ideas of how much training it would need to become Batman, and if it's even possible to become him in real life.

1362. Turophobia is the fear of cheese.

1363. Based on two different studies performed by researchers, it was concluded that people who drink their coffee black or bitter are more associated with antisocial personality traits and sadism.

1364. Casinos are mostly designed in a way to avoid people from turning at a ninety degree angle when they walk. Author Natasha Dow Schull, who wrote "Addiction by Design, Machine Gambling in Las Vegas," states in her book that making these sharp turns forces people to activate the decision-making part of their brains. Hence casinos want you to curve gently when you walk through them.

1365. During the 2000 Summer Paralympics Games, Spain cheated by making everyone believe that ten out of the twelve players on their roster were mentally disabled, when they actually had no disability at all.

1366. Margarine is naturally white. When it was first introduced, thirty two states had imposed color constraints on it. Vermont, New Hampshire, and South Dakota all passed laws demanding that margarine be dyed pink. Other states proposed it be colored red, brown, or black. The reason behind it was that butter makers didn't want it to be yellow, as it was already the color of butter.

1367. In an effort to reduce rampant speeding in Arnprior, Scotland, local authorities had the lines on the road repainted to look wiggly. The twisting lines haven't reduced the speeding, but they have really upset local residents.

1368. Due to the way that horse legs are built, they can actually sleep while standing up. Their legs have ligaments and a structure that allows them to doze off without collapsing.

1369. Originally, Spider-Ham was a spider named "Peter" who was bitten by a radioactive pig, not the other way around.

1370. In 1985, a hospital collapsed after a magnitude eight earthquake hit Mexico City. Four new born babies were trapped and survived for a week under rubble. They are known as the miracle babies as they survived without human contact, nourishment or water for seven days.

1371. On January 22, 1943, the world record for the fastest temperature change was registered in Spearfish, South Dakota. The temperature rose from negative four degrees Fahrenheit (twenty degrees Celsius) to forty four degrees Fahrenheit (seven degrees Celsius) in the span of two minutes when the Chinook winds passed through. After the wind passed, the temperature dropped back down to negative four degrees Fahrenheit (twenty degrees Celsius) in just twenty seven minutes. The phenomenon caused glass windows to crack.

1372. The top selling product at Walmart is bananas. The company sells around 999,102,136 pounds (453,592,370 kilograms) of bananas per year worldwide. That's 31.9 pounds (14.5 kilograms) every second of the day.

1373. As a self-defense mechanism, the horned lizard has blood-filled sinuses within the eye sockets that squirt blood by swelling and rupturing.

1374. Based on research conducted at the University of California, in Berkeley, girls who are exposed to chemicals in toothpaste, make up, soap, and other personal care products, may reach puberty earlier than boys, as the chemicals contained in these products speed up the process.

1375. The largest individually produced flower in the world is the Rafflesia Arnoldi plant. It grows more than 35.8 inches (ninety one centimeters) across and weighs almost 24.2 pounds (eleven kilograms).

1376. In 1910, the first ever in-flight radio transmission was sent by Walter Wellmen, while he flew across the Atlantic Ocean along with five companions and his cat. The message said: "Roy, come and get this goddamn cat!"

1377. On February 5, 1869, the world's largest gold nugget ever was found near Denali, Victoria, in Australia. It weighed 159 pounds (seventy two kilograms) and measured two feet by one foot (0.6 by 0.3 meters). It was shipped to the bank of England after melting it into ingots.

1378. In England, all swans are legal property of the Queen.

1379. Research conducted in 2012 by the Monell Chemical Sense Center, shows that steak and wine taste great together because they are on opposite ends of the culinary sensory spectrum, a contrast that's pleasing to the palate.

1380. Beatles band member George Harrison wrote a letter to actor Mike Meyers expressing how much he loved watching the Austin Powers movie, and that turned out to be his last letter.

1381. Wild pigs are considered as one of the most destructive animals in America. They destroy crops, feast on livestock, terrorize tourists, and force other wildlife to flee their homes. They cause more than $400 million in damage each year in Texas alone.

1382. In 2015, a man named Torkel Kristoffers was arrested for kidnapping. It turned out that his neighbors didn't recognize him with his new beard that he grew while taking time off of work, so they alerted the authorities as soon as they saw a stranger getting into Torkel's place.

1383. There is a cafe in Hong Kong called "Rabbit Land." It has bunnies that customers can pet, most of which were abandoned by their previous owners. It caters to people who don't have space for their own rabbit.

1384. If swimming on the moon were possible, you could walk on the water's surface and jump out of the water like a dolphin.

1385. A Russian folk song from the 19th century about a meeting between a peddler and a young girl is actually the theme song for the game Tetris. In the song, he offers the girl his wares and goods in exchange for a kiss.

1386. During the American Civil War, some soldiers had wounds that glowed blue. These soldiers had a better survival rate compared to others, so the glow was called "Angel's Glow." The luminescence was actually due to bacteria that produced antibiotics that live inside nematodes, and these nematodes have made homes in the soldiers' open wounds.

1387. "The Licktators," a London based ice cream company, teamed up with breast-feeding campaigner Victoria Hilly to celebrate the birth of royal baby number two by relaunching their breast milk flavored ice cream. Called the Royal Baby Gaga, the ice cream is made of donated breast milk that has been screened with hospital standards, and Madagascan vanilla.

1388. Notorious Roman Emperor Caligula loved his horse so much that he had a marble stall in an ivory manger. In fact, he wanted to appoint the horse to the High Office of Consul, as an expression of his absolute power, but he was killed before he could do it.

1389. Toldo was a loyal cat from Northeast Italy who visited the grave of his dead owner for more than a year, at times bringing gifts like plastic cups and twigs.

1390. An Ecuadorian artist named Oscar Santillan removed an inch (2.5 centimeters) off England's highest mountain in 2015. Oscar was accused of vandalism and the British demanded that he return the stolen inch.

1391. Al Capone was in the business of used furniture, at least according to the business card that he carried around. Whenever he encountered law enforcement authorities, the gangster would hand out his card, and explain that he was merely a second-hand furniture seller.

1392. In February 2016, a license plate was auctioned off in Hong Kong for $2.3 million. It has the lucky number 28 which sounds like the words "easy" and "to prosper" in Cantonese. For this reason, the number is thought to bring good fortune to the owner.

1393. Oxygen masks in airplanes aren't actually connected to an oxygen tank. They instead use a chemical reaction to generate it on the spot.

1394. Gustave Eiffel, the designer of the Eiffel Tower, added a secret compartment near the top where he would entertain members of the science community.

1395. A child prodigy named Ruth Lawrence was accepted into Oxford University at the age of ten when she passed the entrance exam and came first out of over five hundred students. She graduated two years later with a bachelors degree and earned a doctorate's degree when she was only seventeen.

1396. "Globe Chase Tag" is actually a competitive international league for the popular game "Tag You're It."

1397. Mike Tyson, the legendary heavyweight boxing champion, was taking a tour of the zoo in 1989 with Robin Gibbons, his wife at the time, when he saw an alpha male gorilla harassing other apes. Tyson asked the zookeeper to let him into the cage so he could fight the gorilla. The zookeeper declined, even after Tyson offered him $10,000.

1398. The Great Pacific Garbage Patch, or the Pacific Trash Vortex, is a collection of garbage found in the north part of the Pacific Ocean, made of tiny particles of plastic that never degrade. It spans waters from the west coast of North America all the way to Japan.

1399. To keep with the continuity, naturalist Sir David Attenborough always wears a blue shirt and khaki pants in his specials, as they can sometimes film thousands of miles and months apart.

1400. William Morrison was a dentist who invented cotton candy, something notoriously bad for your teeth.

1401. Caucasians tend to get gray hair first, followed by Asians then African-Americans. Scientists still don't know why.

1402. Before modern refrigeration existed, people in Russia and Finland used to put Russian brown frogs in their milk to keep it fresh. According to organic chemist A.T. Lebedev, from the

147

Moscow State University, the frog's skin secretions are loaded with peptides and anti-microbial compounds.

1403. The world's first hot air balloon trip occurred in September, 1783, in Versailles, France. The passengers however were a rooster, a duck and a sheep, not human beings.

1404. Before manufacturing mobile phones, Nokia Corporation originally manufactured pulp and paper, including toilet paper.

1405. Some people refer to cranberries as bounce berries because they actually bounce when they are ripe.

1406. According to Oxfam, 70% of all clothes that are donated worldwide go to the African continent.

1407. Ryan Gosling and Rachel McAdams didn't like each other when filming The Notebook. But after finishing filming the movie, they fell in love and dated for four years.

1408. In the small town of El Valle de Anton, Panama, there are trees growing that have square trunks, a strange phenomenon of nature that it's believed doesn't occur anywhere else in the world. In fact, experts from the University of Florida took a few tree seedlings and planted them in other locations. The trees didn't retain their rectangular shape and had normal, circular trunks.

1409. There is a picture of a kingfisher diving into water without making a splash. It was taken by wildlife photographer Alan McFadyen after spending 420 hours and taking 720 thousand photos over a six year period.

1410. Western hairstyles that included ponytails, mullets, and elaborate spikes were banned by the Iranian government in 2010.

1411. If you want to be an actor in a zombie movie, you actually have to go to zombie school where you're marked on whether you're a convincing zombie or not.

1412. In 1881, dentist Alfred Southwick witnessed a weird accident when an intoxicated man died after he accidentally touched a live generator terminal. From there he got the idea for the electric chair.

1413. Although camels are thought to live in Australia as an invasive species, some aboriginal recall seeing them in earlier times.

1414. According to Dr. Jeffery Kuhn from the University of Hawaii, the sun is the most perfect sphere ever observed in nature.

1415. Green bell peppers are just less mature, less ripe versions of red, orange, and yellow peppers.

1416. The official state animal of California is the grizzly bear. It was designated as such in 1953, more than thirty years after the last one was killed. It was also honored on the state flag.

1417. There are only three Northern White Rhinos left in the world as of June 2018. One male and two other females live in captivity in Northern Kenya. Sadly, despite this, these creatures are still sought after for their horns by poachers.

1418. The foggiest place in the world is the Grand Banks, in Newfoundland, Canada, with 206 foggy days every year.

1419. A man named László Polgár created a method to raise child prodigies. Later on, he wrote a book on it, married a language teacher, and they both raised the world's best and second-best chess players.

1420. Lightning usually strikes the same place repeatedly, particularly if it's a tall, pointy, isolated object. The Empire State building, for example, is hit on average twenty three times a year by lightning.

1421. Spain offers citizenship to the descendants of those Spanish people who came to the Americas running away from the Inquisition.

1422. Over the course of years, thousands of satellites have been launched into space amongst meteors, but only one has been hit and destroyed: the European Space Agency Communications Satellite Olympus.

1423. Since 2010, Japanese population has shrunk by one million people; as a result, the government has started to set up speed-dating events. According to economists, younger generations are losing interest in getting married and starting a family.

1424. In 1990, disabled activists left their wheelchairs behind and crawled up the steps of the Capitol. The protest aimed to encourage a vote on the Americans with Disabilities Act.

1425. The coco de mer is the largest fruit in the world and it belongs to the palm tree family. The fruit weighs about 92.5 pounds (forty two kilograms) while the seed weighs 37.4 pounds (seventeen kilograms). It's also known as the sea coconut or the double coconut.

1426. In 1937, author J.R.R. Tolkien started to write "Lord of the Rings." He finally published them in 1955, eighteen years later after having started.

1427. The small tropical archer fish has been taught to accurately recognize human faces. When researchers at the University of Oxford displayed two faces side by side on a screen over a fish tank, one familiar and one unknown, the fish was able to recognize the same face 81% of the time in color, and even more accurately in black and white images.

1428. On June 9, 1946, the first car television commercial was aired. It was for Chevrolet.

1429. On average, people who smoke can die ten years earlier than non-smokers according to the Centers for Disease Control and Prevention. Additionally, for every person who dies because of smoking, at least thirty people suffer from a severe smoking related illness.

1430. Poppy seed consumption can actually produce positive results during drug screening tests.

1431. The smallest spider in the world, according to the Guinness World Records, is the Patu marplesi, also known as the Samoan moss spider. With a body length of only 0.09 inches (0.25 millimeters), this spider belongs to the group of forty four "midget" species that create the smallest spider webs.

1432. Madden NFL, the video game franchise, is older than half the players who currently play in the NFL today.

1433. The most googled person in 2016 was President Donald Trump, not only in the United States, but also in more than eighty eight countries, from India to Mexico to Belgium.

1434. The country with the highest rate of recycled bottles in the world is Finland where over 90% of plastics and cans are recycled and almost 100% of glass bottles are recycled.

1435. In 1987, there were only twenty seven California Condors worldwide. All of them were captured for captive breeding and now, as of 2018, there are 488 of them.

1436. The American company Creative Home Engineering specializes in making hidden rooms for your home. There is a room that even requires a chess board played in a certain combination in order to unlock the room.

1437. Actor Tom Cruise, who is also a Scientology front man, split up with all his three ex-wives Nicole Kidman, Mimi Rogers, and Katie Holmes when they turned thirty three. The number thirty three is considered the "master teacher" in the scientology faith, and it represents true love, altruism, and increased positive energy.

1438. Actor Chuck Norris and Bob Barker, the iconic host of "The Price is Right," have trained karate together for eight years.

1439. Eugene Cernan was the last astronaut to walk on the moon. In December, 1972, before he got back into the lander, he used his foot to write the initials TDC over the dusty moon surface. They represented the names of his daughter Tracy, and in theory, they are still written on the moon today.

1440. In 2000, Justin Timberlake's leftover French toast was actually sold on eBay. Nineteen year old Kathy Summers paid $1,025 for it. The famous singer finished a breakfast interview at the studio of New York area radio station Z100, and the DJ put it on eBay shortly after he left.

1441. When the menstrual pad was first invented, it was held up by a belt.

1442. The first politician to ever use political TV ads was presidential candidate Dwight D. Eisenhower, during his 1952 campaign. He created forty twenty-second TV ads where he answered questions from the audience.

1443. Russian ice slides from the 17th century were actually the inspiration for the modern rollercoaster. They were tall, wooden structures with ice frozen over a long, sloping ramp; they used to rise up over seventy nine feet (twenty-four meters) with ramps that stretched for hundreds of meters; the ice sleds were simply a block of ice with a straw mat.

1444. In 2017, the celebration of Valentine's Day was banned in Pakistan by the Islamabad High Court.

1445. The final words of murderer Gary Gilmore actually inspired

Nike's slogan, Just Do It. Before being executed by firing squad, his final words were "let's do it." Advertising executive Dan Wieden modified it and pitched it to Nike, creating their iconic slogan.

1446. Donald Trump describes himself as a philanthropist, however, he ranks as one of the least charitable billionaires in the entire world.

1447. The reason why all cruise ships contain morgues is because about 200 people die while at sea every year, hence they need somewhere on the ship to be stored.

1448. The only person to have won British Academy of Film and Television Arts Awards in black and white, color, HD, 3-D, and 4k was broadcaster and national historian Sir David Attenborough.

1449. In Cleveland, there is a system where college students get to live for free at retirement houses as it's mutually beneficial for both parties. The retirees get contact with younger people where studies have shown helps beat dementia and the students save on housing costs.

1450. 105-year-old French cyclist Robert Marchand set a world record on January 4, 2017, for the longest distance cycled in one hour at the Velodrome just outside of Paris. The record was set in the 105+ age category, which was created especially for him. He rode almost fourteen miles (twenty three kilometers) in an hour.

1451. Tonic immobility is a trance-like state where sharks fall when they are flipped upside down. Orcas have figured this out and have been seen in the wild turning great whites over and killing them. It became one of the few instances of something else preying on great white sharks instead of humans.

1452. The African Union is planning to have a single continent-wide currency modeled after the Euro. The most popular proposed name for the currency is the "Afro."

1453. Throwing a penny from the top of the Empire State Building would not be lethal to anyone on the ground as it's too small and flat. According to physicist Louis Bloomfield from the University of Virginia, if a penny landed on someone from that height, then it would feel more like getting flicked and not even that hard.

1454. A group of mallard ducks were studied and filmed when they were sleeping in a row by researchers at Indiana State University. Scientists found that the ducks on the end of each row had one eye open and half of their brains were still functioning. The reason why was to keep a good look-out for predators and other potential threats to their group.

1455. Back in the 1600's, tulips used to be the most expensive flower. They were even more valuable than most people's homes and cost nearly ten times what the average working man would earn in a whole year.

1456. About half of Australia's koalas have chlamydia, which can also infect humans.

1457. 40% of pregnant women develop gingivitis at some point during their pregnancy as a result of varying hormone levels. This condition is called "pregnancy gingivitis."

1458. Bill Morgan, an Australian truck driver, is one of the luckiest people alive. He was involved in a near-fatal truck accident and had a heart attack. He was clinically dead for more than fourteen minutes and survived; he then was in a coma for twelve days and made his way out of it. He then won the lottery twice. With the first winning ticket, he won a car worth $17,000; and during a reenactment for a Melbourne TV show, he purchased another ticket and won a jackpot of $170,000.

1459. In the late summer and fall, blue jays and cardinals go bald. Sometimes they lose all their feathers gradually; sometimes they lose them all at once. They are only bald for about a week until their feathers grow back.

1460. In Bavaria, Germany, the medieval town of Nordlingen is situated entirely inside a meteorite crater. It's 15.5 miles (twenty five kilometers) across and it's estimated to have formed 14.5 million years ago.

1461. Rats have a really strong sense of smell and have been able to detect buried landmines in the past. For this reason, the US Fish and Wildlife Service is testing the African Giant Pouched Rat to see whether it can help detect illegal shipments of hardwood timber, part of a multi-billion dollar black market industry, as well as pangolins, the world's most poached mammal.

1462. The Tropical Island Resort in Krausnick, Germany, is the world's largest indoor beach. It was built inside an old airplane hangar and has a 50,000-plant forest that spans over a 107,000 square foot (9,940 square meter) area; it has a spa, a waterfall, a whirlpool, and a water slide. In fact, the indoor is so big that it's possible to fly a hot air balloon inside.

1463. Even though slavery was abolished in the United States in 1865, there was a family of slaves working in rural Louisiana until 1961.

1464. Before his assassination in 1968, Robert Kennedy had eleven children with his wife Ethel. They also had thirty five grandchildren.

1465. Scientists from Georgia State University have found that monkeys are susceptible to optical illusions, just like humans. To test this, Capuchin and Rhesus monkeys looked at a visual illusion where two dots were surrounded by rings, but were actually the same size, and they were tricked much like many people were.

1466. According to neuroscientist Glen Jeffrey from the University College London, the eye color of reindeer changes depending on the time of the year. In the summer they turn golden, reflecting more light through the retina, which helps them deal with the almost continuous Arctic summer daylight. However, in the winter, they turn a deep blue to help them deal with the almost continuous winter darkness.

1467. In 2015, a gigantic cloud of methyl alcohol, also called methanol, surrounding a stellar nursery was discovered by astronomers; it measured over 310 billion miles (500 million kilometers) across. In the future, it could help astronomers understand how some of the most massive stars in the universe are formed.

1468. Mel Gibson, who has won two Oscars, has a rare birth defect which affects about one in 600 newborns called horseshoe kidney. His two kidneys fused before he was born, forming a horseshoe or U-shape.

1469. In 2010, the UN Environment Programme released a report stating that from 150 to 200 species of plants, insects, birds, and mammals go extinct every twenty four hours, which is about 1,000 times faster than the natural rate. According to biologists, the world has not seen a mass extinction like this since the end of the dinosaurs, which was about sixty five million years ago.

1470. There are some traffic lights in Germany that have touch screens installed where you can play pong with pedestrians across the street from you.

1471. The shortest commercial flight in the world is only 1.7 miles (2.73 kilometers) in distance. It covers the way between two small Orkney Islands north of Scotland, from the Westray Airport to the Papa Westray Airport. If the wind is ideal, it can take as little as forty seven seconds from start to finish.

1472. In Sarasota, Florida, they have an Amish beach called "Pinecraft," which allows folks who like a simpler life to take in the sun on the sand while sticking with their traditional values and lifestyle choices. It's a literal Amish paradise, and probably the only one of its kind anywhere in the world.

1473. The Mama Zebra Program is a project developed in Bolivian cities where a team of young people dress in zebra costumes and dance in the streets to make drivers and pedestrians aware of traffic rules. The zebra was picked because of the pattern of the zebra crossing.

1474. In 1891, electricity was first introduced to the White House. The then President Benjamin Harrison and his wife refused to touch any of the light switches because they were afraid of being electrocuted, so they had employees follow them around the White House to turn the switches on and off for them whenever they entered or left a room.

1475. Kowloon Walled City in China existed from 1810 to 1993. Before the city was demolished, it was controlled by triads with thousands of people involved in drugs, gambling, and prostitution.

1476. In 1597, a three part book about necromancy and demonology was written and published by King James the first of England.

1477. The Asian arowana, also known as the dragon fish, is the world's most expensive aquarium fish. The Chinese believe that they bring good luck and prosperity due to its red color and coin-like scales. This fish has sold for up to $300,000.

1478. An April fool's Day joke turned awry in 2013 when two DJs in Florida told fans that their taps were emitting dihydrogen monoxide. This resulted in serious panic, and the DJs were suspended until they paid a fine. The funny part is that dihydrogen monoxide is actually supposed to come out of taps and is just a different way to say water.

1479. The seven rays found on the Statue of Liberty's crown represent the seven continents. Each ray measures nine feet (2.7 meters) long and weighs as much as 150 pounds (sixty eight kilograms). Additionally, its overall height is 305 feet (ninety two meters) from its base, and it has a thirty five foot (ten meters) waistline and weighs 225 tons.

1480. According to a study published in the Journal of Current Biology, people who exercise four hours after learning something new retained the information better two days later than those who exercise immediately or not at all.

1481. The only US state that considers cannibalism illegal is Idaho. In fact, a ban was created in 1990 after spreading fear that cannibalism would present itself in ritualized practices.

1482. The most popular fruit in the world is tomato.

1483. Scorpions can live under extreme temperatures. They can even survive being frozen and thawed and extreme heat up to 122 degrees Fahrenheit (fifty degrees Celsius).

1484. It's possible for the praying mantises to turn their heads 180 degrees. This ability helps them scan their surroundings using two large, compound eyes and three other simple eyes located between them.

1485. On January 19, 1977, it snowed in South Florida for the first time in recorded history. Jim Lushine, a retired meteorologist, thought that cocaine was falling from the sky after perhaps a bad drug drop had gone bad.

1486. The letter "I" in Apple products, such as iPod, iPad, and iMac, stands for Internet. When the iMac was first introduced in 1998 by Steve Jobs, he explained this.
1487. An old slang term for moonshine is Mountain Dew.
1488. Most mammals don't live long after their reproductive years are over. Only a few do, such as the killer whale, pilot whales, human beings, and some great apes.
1489. Some scientists believe that our planet used to have two moons orbiting it. The little moon crashed into the bigger moon, creating the one moon that we know and love. They believe this because the far side of the moon is very different from the near side, which might indicate that the far side was changed by the collision that scarred it.
1490. Research in 2014 showed that the average football player runs seven miles (11.2 kilometers) each game.
1491. Harrison Ford used to be a carpenter prior to becoming a superstar actor. He was working for famous producer Fred Roos, fixing a door in a location where George Lucas was holding casting meetings for Star Wars. He randomly auditioned for the role of Han Solo, got the part, and shortly after became famous.
1492. Throughout Phoenix, Arizona, wild parrots have been spreading and seen for years. Conservationist Greg Clark remarked that these colonies were started in the 1980's when an aviary released a hundred birds after a monsoon. He also pointed out that another aviary released more birds around that time because the owner didn't want them anymore.
1493. Because of a toothache, a Swedish inmate escaped from prison in 2013 and went to a dentist to get it fixed. After the pain was treated, he turned himself back into the police. His sentence of one month was only increased by a day.
1494. In the 1984 movie "Indiana Jones and the Temple of Doom," the name of the bar in the opening fight scene is Club Obi Wan. The name was based on the character Obi-Wan Kenobi from the "Star Wars" films, also directed by George Lucas.
1495. The university that has produced the greatest number of

billionaires in the world is the University of Pennsylvania with twenty five billionaires.

1496. New Zealand doesn't issue residency visas to people with high BMI; there have even been cases of people rejected just because of their weight.

1497. In 1999, Olle Terenius, from the Swedish University of Agricultural Sciences, found out that mute swans can windsurf across water. When these birds want to go fast, they put up their wings and tails to catch a breeze.

1498. "Got It" is a Silicon Valley-based company that has developed an app with the same name. If a student gets stuck on a question, they can submit it to the app and get tutors to bid for an answer. When the student accepts the bid, which generally costs about a dollar, they get a ten-minute long tutoring session by text.

1499. Out of all the peaches in the world, China is responsible for producing 58%. With a worldwide production of twenty five million metric tons, that represents about 14.4 million metric tons.

1500. In the Vietnamese version of Cinderella, known as "Tam Cam," Cinderella cuts her stepsister into pieces, puts the pieces into a jar of food, and sends it to her stepmother to eat, who enjoys it until she finds a skull at the bottom of the jar, and then dies out of shock.

AFTERWORD

Did you enjoy the book or learn something new? It really helps out small publishers like Scott Matthews if you could leave a quick review on Amazon so others in the community can also find the book!